NEW MUSIC VOCABULARY
A Guide to Notational Signs for Contemporary Music

NEW MUSIC VOCABULARY

A Guide to Notational Signs
for Contemporary Music

HOWARD RISATTI

UNIVERSITY OF ILLINOIS PRESS
Urbana Chicago London

Library of Congress Cataloging in Publication Data

Risatti, Howard, 1943-
  New music vocabulary.

  Bibliography: p.
  1. Musical notation. I. Title.
ML431.R6   781'.24   73-81565
ISBN 0-252-00406-X

CONTENTS

FOREWORD

This book has come into being because of the need for composers and performers, as well as musicologists, to have a "dictionary" of the notational invention of the last few decades.
Even today, in the past (almost) quarter of the century, it is not uncommon to find performers who have never encountered any of the signal devices found in these pages, and consequently have no idea as to intended performance practice. Young composers, too, have, in instances, not encountered much of this notational invention. Thus, when facing compositional problems of a unique nature, they will often invent their own notation, thereby proliferating the problems of quantity and interpretation of new symbols.
The material here was gathered under my supervision for a special topics course in Music at the University of Illinois. At the inception of the project, neither Howard Risatti nor I anticipated the great amount of material that we would find. More than 600 scores were examined: even so, it is quite likely that some items are not included, or that some composer's individual usage for a symbol is not described.
An evaluation of the superiority of one notational system over another has not been attempted here for several reasons: To begin with, it is hard to be totally objective since familiarity with a particular set of symbols makes that set more stimulating than another set which is unfamiliar. Then, too, written music has always been simply visual information to the performer. Any device is useful and valid that enables a performer to represent accurately the composer's ideas to the listener, or that conveys on the page the composer's ideas to the reader.
If the past can be any indication of the future, then those symbols and devices that most effectively convey their meanings will be retained, while the less effective symbols will disappear, as is already being observed.
For those of us that specialize in the performance or study of the newest music, there is very little in these pages that is startling or unusual. But for those others who are just discovering this musical world, herein lies a wealth of information and clarification.

Paul Zonn

PREFACE

It has been the intent of the author to make readily available
a considerable body of contemporary notational material in
order to show the logical growth of present-day musical ideas,
as well as to offer a source list of symbols and ideas for
student and composer alike. The proliferation of notational
signs for modern music is directly related to the exploration
of new sound-production techniques on traditional instruments.
As these new techniques become standardized, the need for in-
venting new symbols will decrease. It is already evident that
the sixties comprised a decade of musical discovery. The sev-
enties promise to be a time of synthesis and development.

Through acquaintance with the symbols and ideas used by
the many modern composers, it is hoped that the common ground
may be recognized and expanded to allow the growth and development of a standardized notational vocabulary.

ACKNOWLEDGMENTS

I am indebted to Paul Zonn of the University of Illinois for his help in the preparation of this book, especially for his suggestions and advice on technical material and for the use of his library and scores in his possession.

I should also like to thank Ramon Zupko from Western Michigan University for reading Chapters II, III, IV, and V of the manuscript. The tedious process of securing material and scores was greatly lessened by the generous help of John and Kathy Klaus of George Washington College in Charlestown, Maryland.

To my wife Michaeline who, along with my brother J. Bruno, read and corrected the finished draft,

My kindest thanks,

H.R.

INTRODUCTION: ORGANIZATION OF MATERIAL

This book has been organized into six chapters: Chapter I surveys general material pertinent to many instruments; succeeding chapters deal with one of the instrumental groups, and the sixth and final chapter deals with voice.

The instrumental chapters have been arranged so that the material which pertains to the instrumental group is presented first, and is followed by terminology or symbols pertinent to individual instruments of the group. These notational signs are listed under the heading for the specific instrument.

Alphabetical sequence of terms has been followed whenever possible, and the material under each heading is arranged so that the more precise symbols precede the less precise. It should be stressed that with the various notational systems shown in Chapter I it is possible to use almost any sign in several different (and sometimes contrasting) ways. The basic idea behind a sign is presented, and the reader is referred to the literature for further specific uses and examples.

Each sign, except those deemed unnecessary because of widespread usage, is keyed to a number identifying the composer and a letter indicating the name of the composition in which the example or a similar example may be found. The List of Composers Cited, arranged alphabetically by composer and serially numbered, provides the origins for the numbered examples. When two or more compositions are listed for a composer, these have been lettered A, B, C etc. Note that in the text all examples or groups of examples are read from left to right, or from top to bottom as A, B, C etc., whether they are specifically lettered or not. This also applies to List of Composers numberings accompanying the examples.

GENERAL NOTATIONAL MATERIAL

CHAPTER I. GENERAL NOTATIONAL MATERIAL

DURATION

The problem of notation has received considerable attention from contemporary composers, with the result that numerous systems have developed. Each of these systems, dependent upon a musical "style," best expresses that style. This is not to say that each system is mutually exclusive of every other system, but that certain musical techniques fit more easily in some systems than others. Perhaps for this reason, these systems tend not to be absolutely uniform, but share elements with other systems.

In most of these systems a time value is given to a spatial unit. This value is attained by assigning a speed to a measured distance; for instance, one inch of score equals one second, or the material between two arrowheads is to be played at such a speed as to last six seconds: ⟵ 6" ⟶ .
Another method is to indicate units similar to measures and show their duration by placing traditional note values above them with a metronome marking at the beginning of the piece, such as ♩ ♪♩ .

The following examples are approximate transcriptions of the same musical material into various notational systems. Example I is rendered in traditional notation without bar lines or meter. Note that the spacing of the noteheads always approximates the desired rhythm; this is so even in the traditionally notated phrase.

Example I

Duration (cont'd):

According to the Shape of the Notehead

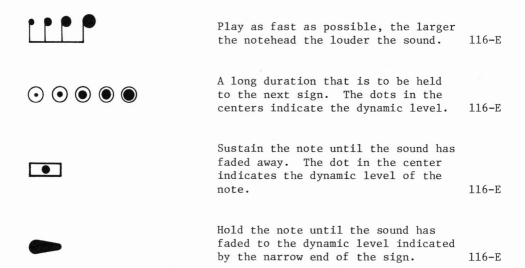

Play as fast as possible, the larger
the notehead the louder the sound.   116-E

A long duration that is to be held
to the next sign. The dots in the
centers indicate the dynamic level.   116-E

Sustain the note until the sound has
faded away. The dot in the center
indicates the dynamic level of the
note.   116-E

Hold the note until the sound has
faded to the dynamic level indicated
by the narrow end of the sign.   116-E

Example II

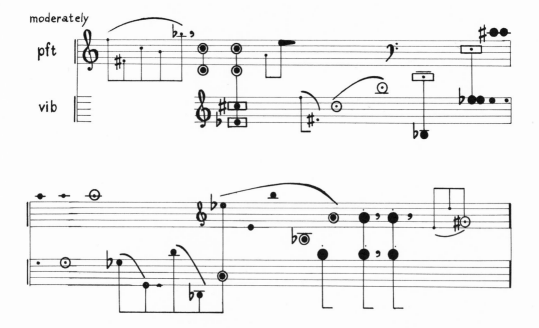

Duration: Notehead Shape (cont'd):

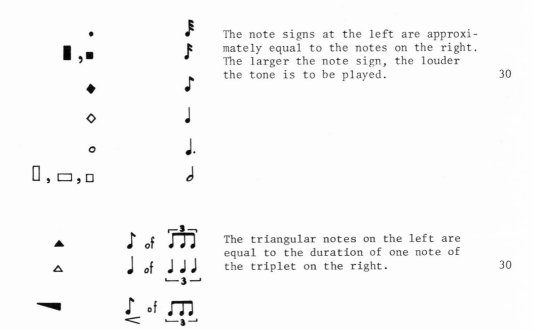

The note signs at the left are approximately equal to the notes on the right. The larger the note sign, the louder the tone is to be played.

30

The triangular notes on the left are equal to the duration of one note of the triplet on the right.

30

Example III

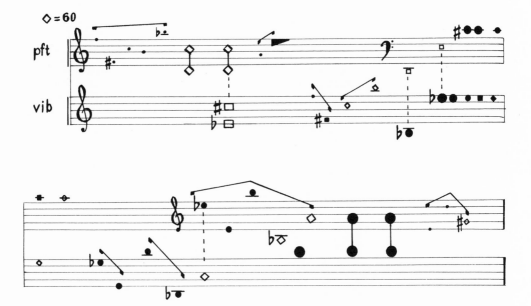

Duration: Notehead Shape (cont'd):

A. A relatively long tone.
B. A relatively short tone.
C. A very short tone.   97-A

A. A very long tone.
B. One half as long as 'A.'
C. One quarter as long as 'A.'   12-C

A. Three seconds long.
B. Two seconds long.
C. One second long.   76

Indeterminate values. The durations
decrease from left to right. These
signs are usually used to denote
freer passages within traditionally
notated phrases or pieces.   2-A

A. A tone of long duration.
B. A tone of short duration.
C. A tone of very short duration.   25-A

The different-sized signs indicate
relative periods of duration. The
larger the sign, the longer the
duration of the sound.   64

Within traditional notation, this type
of note indicates a sound of indeterminate duration.   96-D

A. Long duration.
B. Medium duration.
C. Short duration.   28

A note that is to be played as fast as
possible.   42-A

A note whose duration is one-half to
two seconds long.   42-A

Duration (cont'd):

Proportional Notation

In the following notational system the speed and rhythm of the notes are determined by the amount of space that separates each notehead. In general, traditional note values are used for longer durations: ♩, 𝅗𝅥, o, |o| . It is also common to find extended beaming, extended noteheads, or slurs to indicate the durations of such values.

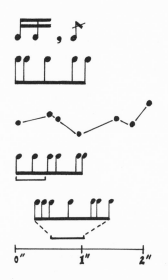

Very fast and short duration.   51-B

Very fast and short duration with the rhythm varied according to the space between the noteheads.   51-B, 57-D, 68

Short durations; the rhythm is deter- mined by the spacing. Play nervously. 51-D

To be played in the rhythm indicated by the spacing, but in the time span of the bracket below the beam.   16-A

105-D

Example IV

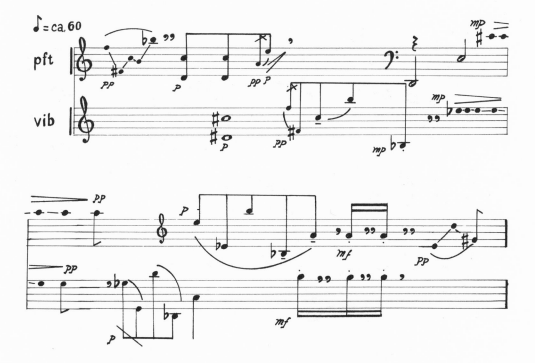

Duration (cont'd):

Traditional Type Beaming

    The use of beaming in the traditional manner is quite common; but here the durations are determined only in relation to the notes themselves— ♪ short, ♫ very short, etc. The more beams a note has, the shorter the duration of the note. Rhythm is determined by the spacing of the noteheads, as in the previous system of notation.

	Fast notes: very short duration.	56
	Not too fast: short duration.	56
	Moderate speed and duration.	56
	A held note.	56

Example V

Duration (cont'd):

Traditional Beaming: Variants

Example VI uses a system of beaming that closely resembles traditional notation, but the durational values are only approximate and the beaming is drawn through the first few stems of each note group.

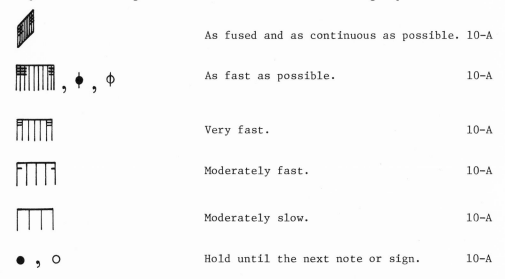

As fused and as continuous as possible. 10-A

As fast as possible. 10-A

Very fast. 10-A

Moderately fast. 10-A

Moderately slow. 10-A

Hold until the next note or sign. 10-A

Example VI

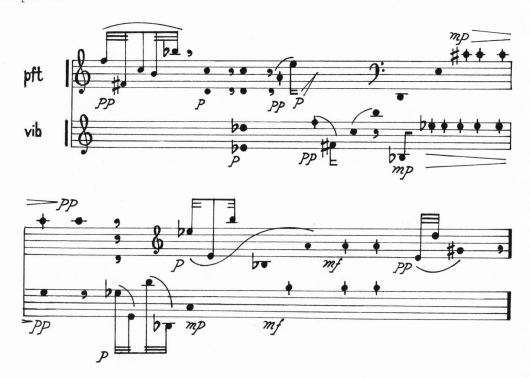

Duration (cont'd):

Beaming Systems: Variants

Rather than multiplying flags or beams, the system below makes use
of a single flag. The durational value is shown by the direction of the
flag and its position on the stem.

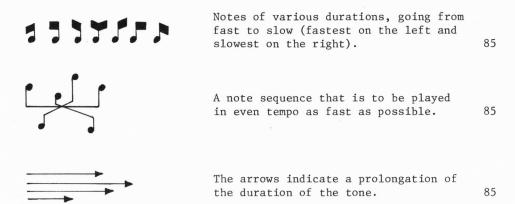

Notes of various durations, going from
fast to slow (fastest on the left and
slowest on the right).   85

A note sequence that is to be played
in even tempo as fast as possible.   85

The arrows indicate a prolongation of
the duration of the tone.   85

Example VII

Duration: Beaming Systems: Variants (cont'd):

Though the system in Example VIII uses traditional beaming, the
beaming does not indicate absolute durational values. The stemless
notes that are shown also signify approximate values, but always of
longer durations.

	As fast as possible.	37-A
	Almost as fast as possible.	37-A
	Very fast.	37-A
	Fast, but not as fast as the small notes with the slash marks (the three examples above).	37-A
	Moderate duration.	37-A
	A little longer duration than above.	37-A
	A long duration.	37-A
	A very long duration.	37-A
	A dotted eighth note.	75

Example VIII

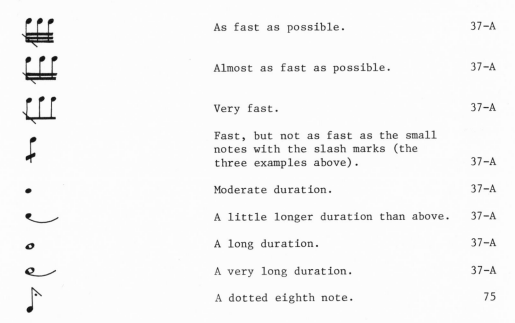

Duration (cont'd):

Beaming Systems: Extended Noteheads

The problems of most durational values are solved by extending the notehead into a horizontal line. Problems do arise with very fast notes; then traditional beaming is used to denote the speed. Rhythm is shown by traditional beaming or by the spacing of the noteheads.

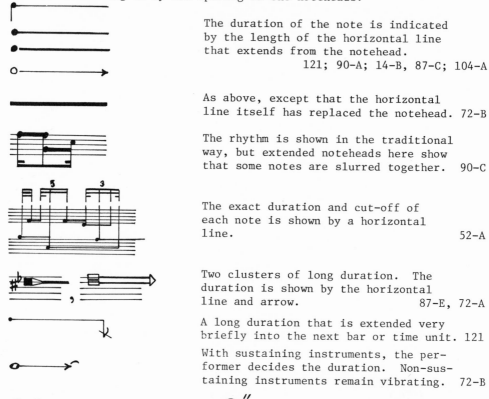

The duration of the note is indicated by the length of the horizontal line that extends from the notehead.
                          121; 90-A; 14-B, 87-C; 104-A

As above, except that the horizontal line itself has replaced the notehead. 72-B

The rhythm is shown in the traditional way, but extended noteheads here show that some notes are slurred together. 90-C

The exact duration and cut-off of each note is shown by a horizontal line.   52-A

Two clusters of long duration. The duration is shown by the horizontal line and arrow.   87-E, 72-A

A long duration that is extended very briefly into the next bar or time unit. 121

With sustaining instruments, the performer decides the duration. Non-sustaining instruments remain vibrating. 72-B

Example IX

Duration (cont'd):

Extended Beams

In this system of notation, the beams are extended into horizontal
lines which continue for the duration of the note. Notes of short duration are represented as notes with short beams; very short notes are
represented either with the traditional beaming, or as notes without
beams or without stems. Rhythm is indicated by the spacing of the noteheads.

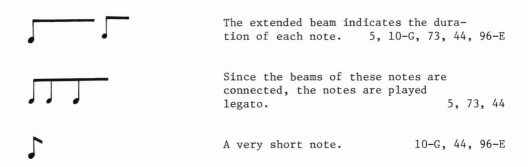

The extended beam indicates the duration of each note.   5, 10-G, 73, 44, 96-E

Since the beams of these notes are
connected, the notes are played
legato.   5, 73, 44

A very short note.   10-G, 44, 96-E

Example X

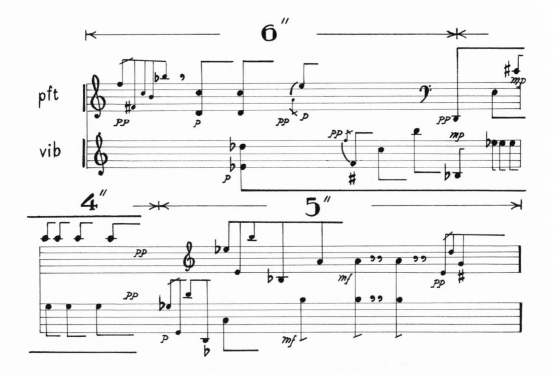

Duration (cont'd):

  Extended Beams: Variations

     A variation of the system of extended beaming is seen in Example
XI, below. Here the beaming indicates not only the durational value,
but also the dynamic value. A thin line signifies a soft tone, and a
thick line signifies a loud tone. Crescendos and decrescendos are
shown by wedge-shaped beams.

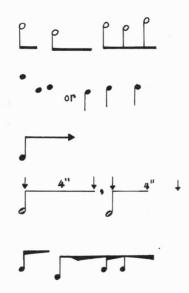

The duration is indicated by the beaming. The open noteheads have no sig-
nificance.   67-A

Very short notes. The rhythm is indicated by the spacing of the noteheads.
                                     67-A, 73

The duration of the sound is left to
the discretion of the performer.   5

Continue the sound for the duration of
the beam:
    A. Four seconds.
    B. Two seconds.   7-B

The duration as well as the dynamics
are indicated by the extended beam.
The thicker the beam, the louder the
sound.   6-A, 109

Example XI

Duration (cont'd):

Slurs

Slurs may be used to notate the length of longer notes by extending them for the desired duration. Shorter notes are notated in the traditional manner. Rhythm is indicated by the spacing of the noteheads or by the use of traditional beaming.

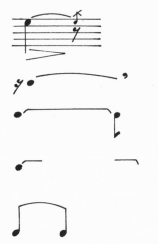

The duration of the tone is extended into the time of the rest for the duration of a grace note. 40

The tone is sustained until the end of the slur sign. 56

The note is held until and/or tied to the following note. 10-G

The note is held until the slur sign is closed. A broken slur is used rather than a complete slur. 100-D

When the stems are connected by a slur, the sound is to sustain until the end of the slur. 116-A

Example XII

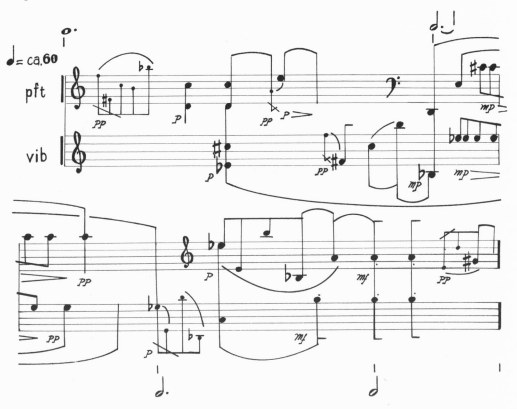

Duration (cont'd):

  Superimposed Indicators

     Superimposed temporal numbers or signs may be used to indicate the
duration of groups of notes, phrases, or single notes. They are usually
used for longer durations and are commonly found in more flexible passages within traditionally notated pieces.

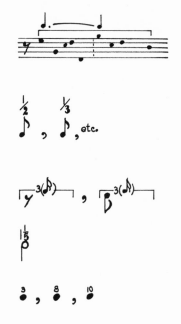

The duration of the bracketed notes
is indicated by the tied notes above
the staff. The rhythm of the stemless notes is in proportion to their
spacing.   34-A

Once a unit or beat has been estab-
lished, the sign determines the note
value in relation to that beat.
  A. Note equals 1/2 beat.
  B. Note equals 1/3 beat.   128-B

The note or rest is equal to 2/3 of
a triplet of 1/16 notes. The re-
maining part of the triplet may be
overlapping another beat.   23-D

The number indicates, in seconds or
beats, the duration of the note.   128-A, 12-B

A number is assigned to the fastest
impulse chosen by the performer. The
other numbers indicate relationships
to that number. (**1** = fastest impulse
or beat.)   93

Example XIII

Duration (cont'd):

Superimposed Indicators: Multiple Usage

The following groups of symbols may be used with various notational systems. They are designed to add a greater degree of flexibility to the values of both notes and rests.

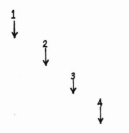

Equals circa

30

A tone or rest of
    A. Very short duration.
    B. Semi-short duration.
    C. Medium duration.
    D. Long duration.
    E. Maximal duration.   21-C

A plus sign indicates a prolonging of the rest. A double plus indicates a greater prolongation, etc.   15-B

A plus after a note also indicates a prolongation of the duration.   72-B, A

The slur indicates that the note or rest is to be held longer than the duration otherwise would be.   72-B, A

Hold the indicated tone for as long as possible. One bow, or one whole breath.   96-E

ACCIDENTALS

1/4 and 3/4 Tone

The following are systems of accidentals used by various composers to signify 1/4 and 3/4 tone alterations of pitch.

Alter the indicated note as shown:

♮+¼ , ♮-¼	1/4 tone up, 1/4 tone down. 62-C
♯or♮ ,♭ or♮ ,♯ ,♭	1/4 up, 1/4 down, 3/4 up, 3/4 down. 57-E, 28, 72-A
↿ ,↾ ,♯↿ ,♭↾	1/4 up, 1/4 down, 3/4 up, 3/4 down. 59-B
↑ ,♭ ,⇈ ,↓	1/4 up, 1/4 down, 3/4 up, 3/4 down. 67-A, 84-E, 89-A
♭ , ♭♭	1/4 down, 3/4 down. 99
↑ ,♭ ,♯♯ ,♭♭	1/4 up, 1/4 down, 3/4 up, 3/4 down. 77
♭	1/4 down. 106
╪ ,↓ ,♯♯ ,♭	1/4 up, 1/4 down, 3/4 up, 3/4 down. 115
↑ , ♯	1/4 up, 3/4 up. 19-C
╪ ,♭	1/4 up, 1/4 down. 119-C, 97-A
╪ ,♭	1/4 up, 1/4 down. 12-C
♯ ,↓ ,♯ ,♭	1/4 up, 1/4 down, 3/4 up, 3/4 down. 15-D
╪ ,♭ ,♯♯ ,♭	1/4 up, 1/4 down, 3/4 up, 3/4 down. 6-A, 99, 9
♯↓ ,♭↓ ,	1/4 up, 1/4 down. 7-B
↑ ♯	1/4 up, 3/4 up. 130-E
↑ , ↓ ,♯♯♯ ,♭	1/4 up, 1/4 down, 3/4 up, 3/4 down. 25-B
↑ , ♭ ,♯	1/4 up, 1/4 down, 3/4 up. 96-E

Accidentals: 1/4 and 3/4 Tone (cont'd):

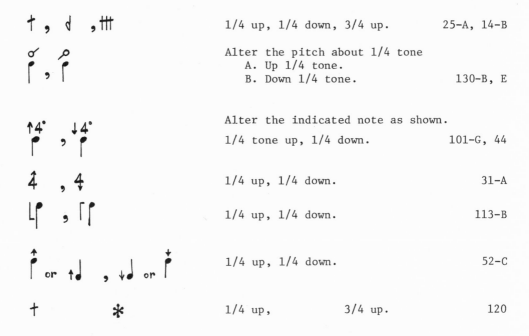

1/4 up, 1/4 down, 3/4 up.		25-A, 14-B
Alter the pitch about 1/4 tone		
A. Up 1/4 tone.		
B. Down 1/4 tone.		130-B, E
Alter the indicated note as shown.		
1/4 tone up, 1/4 down.		101-G, 44
1/4 up, 1/4 down.		31-A
1/4 up, 1/4 down.		113-B
1/4 up, 1/4 down.		52-C
1/4 up,	3/4 up.	120

Accidentals (cont'd):

The following signs show alterations of pitch other than 1/4 and
3/4 tone alterations.

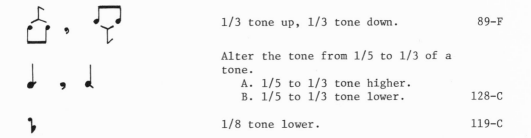

1/3 tone up, 1/3 tone down.	89-F
Alter the tone from 1/5 to 1/3 of a tone.	
A. 1/5 to 1/3 tone higher.	
B. 1/5 to 1/3 tone lower.	128-C
1/8 tone lower.	119-C

Accidentals (cont'd):

Microtonal

The American composer Benjamin Johnston has employed microtonal
variations in pitch by using a system of accidentals based upon the
just-intonation method of tuning. This system is not based on equal-
ly tempered steps and half-steps, but upon justly-tuned major thirds
and perfect fifths. The result is that the corresponding sharps and
flats are not the same pitch.

Accidentals: Microtonal (cont'd):

    The following accidentals have their equivalents given in cents and
may be used in any combination to designate the proper alteration of a
pitch to produce the just-intonation of that pitch.

✕	Raise 140 cents.
♯	Raise 70 cents.
∟	Raise 49 cents.
+	Raise 22 cents.
♭♭	Lower 140 cents.
♭	Lower 70 cents.
⌐	Lower 49 cents.
—	Lower 22 cents.
✕	Raise 91 cents (✕ minus ⌐).
✕	Raise 189 cents (✕ plus ∟).
♯	Raise 119 cents (♯ plus ∟).
♯	Raise 21 cents (♯ minus ⌐).
♭	Lower 119 cents (♭ plus ⌐).
♭	Lower 21 cents (♭ minus ∟). 55

Accidentals (cont'd):

Conventional Sharps and Flats

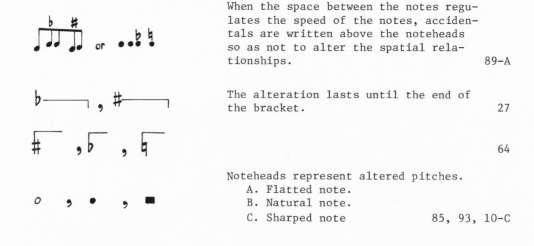

When the space between the notes regu-
lates the speed of the notes, accidentals are written above the noteheads
so as not to alter the spatial relationships.   89-A

The alteration lasts until the end of
the bracket.   27

                                                64

Noteheads represent altered pitches.
    A. Flatted note.
    B. Natural note.
    C. Sharped note   85, 93, 10-C

PITCH

Highest-Lowest Pitch Possible

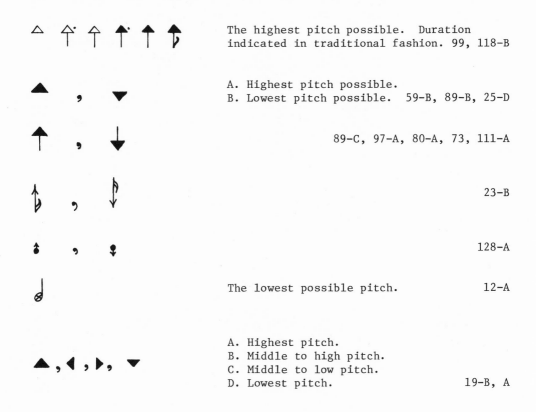

The highest pitch possible. Duration indicated in traditional fashion. 99, 118-B

A. Highest pitch possible.
B. Lowest pitch possible. 59-B, 89-B, 25-D

89-C, 97-A, 80-A, 73, 111-A

23-B

128-A

The lowest possible pitch. 12-A

A. Highest pitch.
B. Middle to high pitch.
C. Middle to low pitch.
D. Lowest pitch. 19-B, A

Pitch (cont'd):

Registers—Pitch Areas

A. Perform within indicated area.
B. Perform above given pitch.
C. Perform below given pitch. 57-D

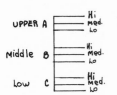

The total pitch range is divided into three areas: A, B, C. These areas are in turn divided into three areas. Pitch is shown by the area in which the note is placed. 84-A

Pitch: Registers-Pitch Areas (cont'd):

In this example, the range is divided
into four areas. Pitches are relative
to each other and to the area in which
they are placed.   73

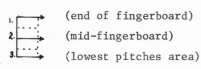

(end of fingerboard)

(mid-fingerboard)

(lowest pitches area)

Pitch ranges are shown in relation to
the body of the instrument.   45

Two examples of divisions of the pitch
range into free, approximate areas.
                        94-B, 100-D, 90-B; 57-C

↑ , ↓

A. The highest register.
B. The lowest register.   67-A

Pitch (cont'd):

  Indefinite Pitches

Perform approximately the indicated
pitch.   57-C

Play in the indicated register, following the pitch contour.   7-B; 10-H

Play in the indicated range, following the pitch contour. Rhythm is
shown by the spacing of the stems.   105-A

Indefinite pitches: let each tone
fade away.   89-B

TEMPO MARKINGS

    Accelerando and Ritardando

♩ = 120 ↔ 130 m.m. , ♩ = 120 ↙ 130	A quarter-note tempo that ranges between 120 and 130 beats/minute.	10-B; 72-B
♩ = 72/76 , ♩ = 72-76	A quarter-note tempo, 72-76 beats /minute.	15-A; 33-A
♩ = 54/60	Choose either of the two tempos.	101-H
♪ ± 60	A half-note tempo that is circa 60 beats/minute.	72-B
♩ = 120 ⟶ 160	A quarter-note tempo that ranges from 120 to 160 beats/minute.	15-B
♪ = MM 80 ↕ MM 63	Choose a tempo between the given limits.	57-D
♩ : 60 ↗72 ↘56	Change tempo freely between the given limits.	48
↙♪ 116 ↗ 〰	The tempo oscillates around 116 beats/minute.	2-B
7/8 subito ♪=82 subito ♪=90 subito ♪=83 ♪ ↓ ↓ ↓ ↓ 2 3 4 6	A rubato, the speed change of which is strictly regulated by the metronome markings.	57-C

Tempo Markings: Accelerando and Ritardando (cont'd):

↑ , ↓

The arrows indicate a sudden tempo
change:
    A. Suddenly quicker.
    B. Suddenly slower.   48

S. , F. , M.

S. = Very slow.
F. = Very fast.
M. = Moderate tempo.   45

The indicated spaces pass at a rate
of forty mm./minute.   10-E

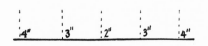

The duration of each space is shown in
seconds. The duration changes according to the number of seconds indicated. 89-E

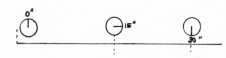

The duration of the space is shown in
seconds on the small clock above the
staff.   61

± **5**″ ——————————————|

The time span of the line is equal to
approximately five seconds.   97-B

⊢ – – + **5**″ – – →| 72-B

Tempo line: the rising line denotes
accelerando, the descending line de-
notes ritardando.   51-E

The tempo marks at the left of the
grid indicate the limits of the accelerando and ritardando of the ris-
ing and falling line.   89-G

Tempo Markings: Accelerando and Ritardando (cont'd):

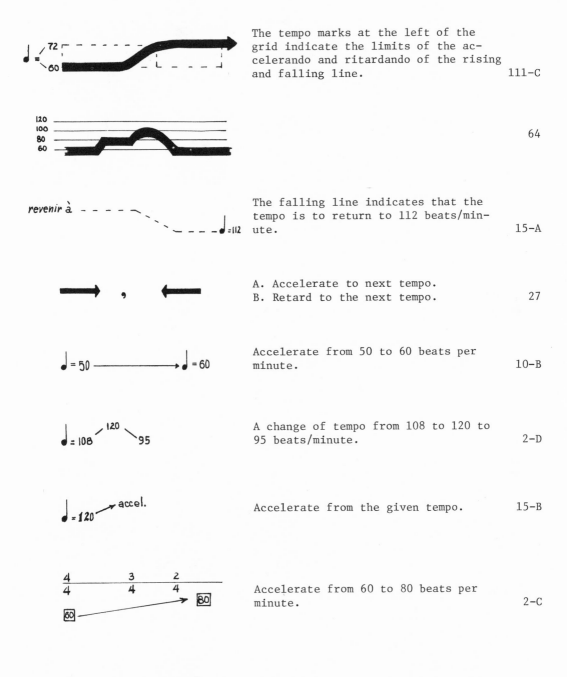

The tempo marks at the left of the grid indicate the limits of the accelerando and ritardando of the rising and falling line.

111-C

64

The falling line indicates that the tempo is to return to 112 beats/minute.

15-A

A. Accelerate to next tempo.
B. Retard to the next tempo.

27

Accelerate from 50 to 60 beats per minute.

10-B

A change of tempo from 108 to 120 to 95 beats/minute.

2-D

Accelerate from the given tempo.

15-B

Accelerate from 60 to 80 beats per minute.

2-C

The rising staff indicates an accelerando. A falling staff would indicate a ritardando.

19-C

ACCELERANDO-RITARDANDO

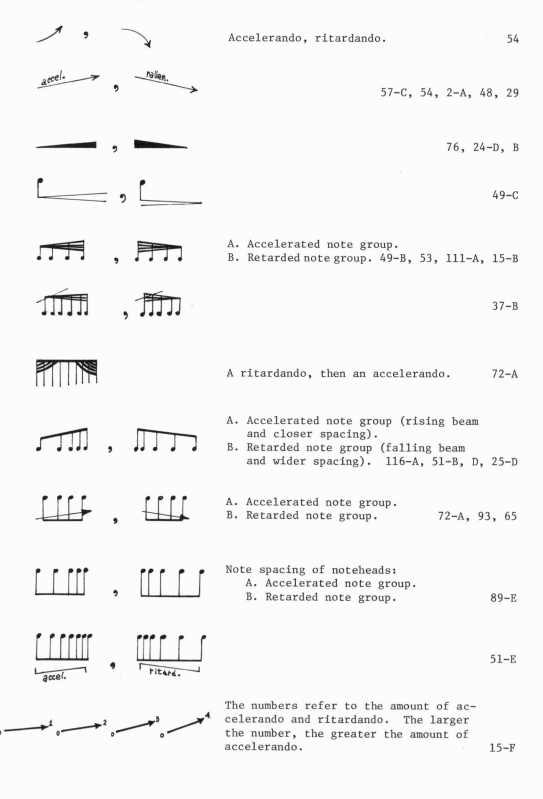

Accelerando, ritardando.   54

57-C, 54, 2-A, 48, 29

76, 24-D, B

49-C

A. Accelerated note group.
B. Retarded note group. 49-B, 53, 111-A, 15-B

37-B

A ritardando, then an accelerando.   72-A

A. Accelerated note group (rising beam
   and closer spacing).
B. Retarded note group (falling beam
   and wider spacing). 116-A, 51-B, D, 25-D

A. Accelerated note group.
B. Retarded note group.   72-A, 93, 65

Note spacing of noteheads:
   A. Accelerated note group.
   B. Retarded note group.   89-E

51-E

The numbers refer to the amount of accelerando and ritardando. The larger
the number, the greater the amount of
accelerando.   15-F

ARPEGGIOS

↑ , ↓ , ↕   A. Arpeggiated upward.
                   B. Arpeggiated downward.
                   C. Arpeggiated in both directions.   57-D

                                                              17, 119-B

▲ , ▼   A. Arpeggiated upward.
                   B. Arpeggiated downward.   116-A

                   Arpeggiated from bottom to top, or
                   from top to bottom, with a break in
                   the continuity of the chord at the
                   point of the arrow and in the direc-
                   tion of the arrow.   51-A

                   A. Slow arpeggio downward.
                   B. Slow arpeggio upward.   17

AMPLIFIED SOUND

● ◑ ○   A. No amplification.
                   B. Half amplified (softly).
                   C. Maximum amplification.   10-I

0. 1. 2. 3.   0 = no amplification.
                   1 = minimum.
                   2 = medium.
                   3 = maximum amplification.   73

+‖‖‖ , ╫╫╫   A. Reverb on.   B. Reverb off.   16-B

   Organized sound interpolation. Instru-
                   ments stop until tape is finished
                   playing.   122-C

CLUSTERS

Accidental above cluster alters all
notes within the cluster unless otherwise specified by an accidental in
front of a notehead.   1

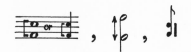

Play all semitones in between the two
tones specified.   73, 106; 104-A; 72-B

118-B

A. Cluster of flatted notes.
B. Cluster of natural notes.
C. Cluster of semitones.   101-H

101-D

A. Semitone cluster without the bottom
   limit indicated.
B. Semitone cluster without the top
   limit indicated.   9

A. Semitone cluster (chromatic
   cluster).
B. Natural note cluster.   25-D

An instrumental cluster in the indicated range. The lower staff shows the
pitch each instrument is to play.
Violin 1 plays pitch number one, VN. 2,
pitch number two, etc.   89-B, E

A cluster made of the highest notes
possible. A footnote gives the number
of pitches. Players agree beforehand
as to which each will play.   89-B

Clusters (cont'd):

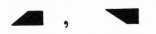
A. Cluster in which lower notes start
   first.
B. Cluster in which top notes start
   first.   101-H

A. Cluster in which lower notes end
   first.
B. Cluster in which top notes end
   first.   101-H

DAMPING AND 'LET VIBRATE'

Let vibrate until tone fades away.
                            48; 111-A; 127

                            96-C; 119-B; 100-D

                            19-B; 72-A

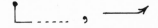
Let vibrate until sound fades away.   6-B

                            90-C

Let sound vibrate until the end of tie
or *.   100-D

VIA indicates point at which vibra-
tions are to stop.   23-B

Damping and 'Let Vibrate' (cont'd):

Let all tones under the bracket vibrate.

51-A

Damp all tones outside of the brackets. 51-A

Triangle indicates the point at which
vibrations are to be damped.   10-H

Damp all sound.   57-C; 10-E; 96-C

105-A; 84-E; 84-E

18; 84-B; 97-A

Damp each tone. The 'V' denotes a
break or silence between the notes.   51-D

Damp only the tone connected to the
tie.   57-C

Choose between damping the tone or
letting it vibrate.   37-B

Damp only the indicated tone (♪).
                                  96-C, 10-E

DYNAMICS

Letters

P/f ,    An asymmetric use of both of the in-
                              dicated dynamics.   51-B; 37-B; 72-B

 , $\frac{mf}{p}$ A. Random, aperiodic use of 'F' and
                                            'P' dynamics.
                                         B. Choice of either 'mF' or 'P.' 42-D; 15-C

$\frac{pp}{f}$ Freely choose within the indicated
                  limits, with the upper dynamic predom-
                  inating.   96-D; 10-H

ⓟ ⓕ   A. Play louder than the dynamic shown.
         B. Play softer than the dynamic shown.   57-E

ⓓ   Freely chosen dynamics.   57-E

P→f , f→P   Freely chosen dynamics, but with an
             over-all increase or decrease of dynam-
             ic clearly heard.   96-D

mf + , p+ , f −   The plus or minus sign indicates a
                   louder or softer dynamic than the
                   letter normally represents.   1

ppp! , fff!   A. As soft as possible.
               B. As loud as possible.   27

P⌐ , P—   The indicated dynamic continues until
           the end of the line.   27; 51-E

ppp s   Always triple piano (s = sempre).   27

ⓕ   The dynamic sign in the circle indi-
         cates that that dynamic level pertains
         to all the tones under the bracket un-
         less otherwise marked.   51-E

$\frac{mp}{f}$ After the conductor has chosen one of
$\frac{p}{pp}$ the pairs of dynamics, the performer
                  is free to choose a dynamic from the
                  indicated pair.   15-C

Dynamics (cont'd):

Crescendo-Decrescendo

	Crescendo to be uniformly played through an unspecified range.	57-E
	Decrescendo through an unspecified range.	57-E
(*pp* <*p*/*f* <*fff*)	A uniform crescendo until midpoint, then increasing steeply to the end.	57-E
(*fff* >*f*/*p* >*ppp*)	Same as above, except decrescendo.	57-E
(*pp*<*ff* <*fff*)	Crescendo steeply at the beginning, then uniformly to the end.	57-E
(*fff* > *pp* > *ppp*)	Same as above, except decrescendo.	57-E
	Continue the rate of increase or decrease uniformly, even through pauses or rests.	57-E
mf ——— +2 -4 ———— *p*	The numbers indicate the relative amount of crescendo or decrescendo.	105-C
p ——— *mf* ——— *p*	A crescendo or decrescendo that follows the contour of the wedges.	15-B
	A. Crescendo. B. Decrescendo. C. Crescendo, then decrescendo. D. Decrescendo, then crescendo.	74, 76 78, 69
	Decrescendo until tone fades away.	24-D
	Decrescendo.	28, 101-C

Dynamics: Crescendo-Decrescendo (cont'd):

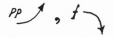

A. Crescendo. B. Decrescendo.	88

The tone under the hold is to start out
'P,' then crescendo.   15-F

Let the vibrations fade until they
reach the indicated dynamic level.   37-B

A vertical crescendo: the higher the
pitch, the louder the note is to be
played.   57-D

                                        15-B, 10-B, 51-E

The dotted line is to insure that the
crescendo does not "leak" into the
next note.   34-A

Dynamics (cont'd):

Accent Marks

sfz , *sffz*

A. Normal sforzando.
B. Loud sforzando.   57-E; 116-E

poco fz , *mfz*

Soft sforzando.   31-A; 12-D

An accent that is delayed until after
the initial attack.   60

∨ , > , < , ∧

∪ , — , > , ∧

⊔ , — , > , ∧

A. Soft accent.   B. Medium accent.
C. Medium loud.   D. Loud accent.
(Note the discrepancy between the 2nd
and 3rd set of examples and the 1st
set of examples.)   85; 15-F; 37-B

The indicated note should slightly
dominate the surrounding notes.   122-D

GRACE NOTES

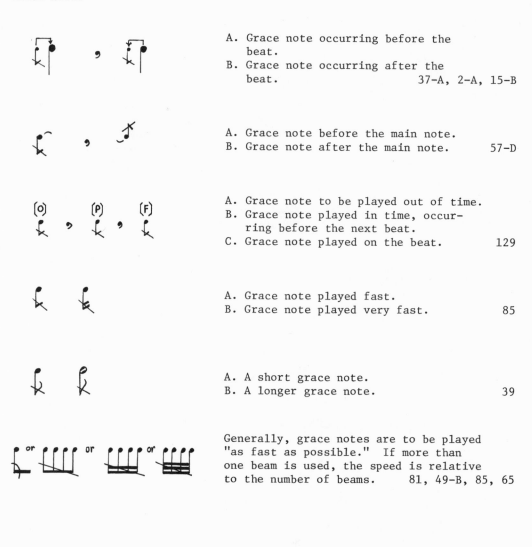

A. Grace note occurring before the beat.
B. Grace note occurring after the beat.   37-A, 2-A, 15-B

A. Grace note before the main note.
B. Grace note after the main note.   57-D

A. Grace note to be played out of time.
B. Grace note played in time, occurring before the next beat.
C. Grace note played on the beat.   129

A. Grace note played fast.
B. Grace note played very fast.   85

A. A short grace note.
B. A longer grace note.   39

Generally, grace notes are to be played "as fast as possible." If more than one beam is used, the speed is relative to the number of beams.   81, 49-B, 85, 65

Play everything under the sign as quickly as possible.   76

Grace notes, the pitches of which are free.   52-C; 38

Very fast quasi grace notes. The pitch is free.   24-B

GLISSANDI

Durations

The noteless stems indicate the beats through which the glissando moves. The grace note shows that the gliss continues through the fourth beat and stops just before the next measure begins. 130-A

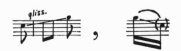

A. The glissando moves through the two eighth notes without heads and ends on the last note.
B. A gliss that ends on the note in parentheses. 41; 15-B

The rests in parentheses show that the duration of the glissando is through these beats. 99

The small note in parentheses shows that the gliss continues through the four time units. 57-B

The tied note shows that the gliss does not start until the last 16th of that beat. The gliss lasts for the duration of 1/16th note. 22-B

The arrow indicates a portamento gliss. That is, a gliss that begins close, both in pitch and time, to the pitch to which it goes. All portamento glissandi are generally of the same time span and frequency interval (ca. 1/2 step), regardless of the interval between the two written notes. 122-B

Glissandi: Durations (cont'd):

The note in parentheses indicates the duration of the portamento gliss.   6-B

A gliss that starts after the rest and ends on the chord that marks the next beat.   71-B

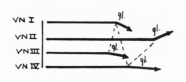

The dotted lines show when and in what order the glissandi are to begin.   89-E

The glissando connects and moves through the indicated pitches.   10-F

Glissandi (cont'd):

Uniform Raising and Lowering of Pitch

Glissando moves from one note to the other without articulating any definite pitches: uniform increase of frequencies like wail of a siren or whistle.   6-B

A uniform gliss that approximates the range indicated by the line.   25-B

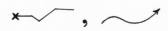

A free gliss in the indicated direction.
96-B; 119-C

Glissandi: Uniform Raising and Lowering of Pitch (cont'd):

Rapid glissandi in the indicated direc-
tion.   96-B; 45

A. Small gliss upward.
B. Small gliss downward.
C. Small gliss either up or down.   21-C

A. An upward gliss to any note.
B. A downward gliss to any note.   14-B

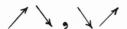

A. A rapid up-and-down gliss.
B. A rapid down-and-up gliss.   105-A, 19-B

A. A gliss from any note to the highest
   note possible.
B. A gliss from any note to the lowest
   note possible.   119-C

A gliss that goes freely through the
indicated pitches.   121

A rapid asymmetrical gliss between the
indicated notes that continues for the
duration of the line.   111-A

A gliss that follows the contour of
the line and is embellished by the
grace notes.   86-A

Glissandi (cont'd):

   Diatonic and Chromatic

A chromatic gliss (gliss based on the chromatic scale) between the indicated notes.   31-A

Chromatic glissandi.   5; 9

A diatonic gliss (gliss based on a diatonic scale).   5

A. Black-note gliss (all sharps or flats).
B. Chromatic gliss.
C. All white-notes gliss (all naturals).
                                        32-A; 116-B

                                                    111-B

Glissandi (cont'd):

   Clusters

A cluster gliss, the pitches of which are indicated on the lower staff (performer 1 = g, performer 2 = g♭, performer 3 = f, etc.).   89-B

A cluster gliss that increases speed in the second and third time units, but slows down in the fourth time unit. 47-C

A gliss formed by turning off the organ with the keys still depressed.   89-C

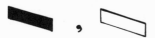

A. Cluster gliss made of all sharped or flatted notes.
B. Cluster gliss of natural notes.   65

Glissandi (cont'd):

1/4 Tone

Gliss by bending the pitch up then down approximately 1/4 tone.　　2-C

A. Bend the pitch down 1/4 tone.
B. Bend the pitch up 1/4 tone.　　6-A

Bend the pitch up about 1/4 tone, then down again.　　43

A gliss up to an 'F' 1/4 tone higher than normal and down to a 'C' 1/4 tone lower than normal.　　122-B

Bend the pitch from 'n' (normal pitch) to flatted pitch, then to sharped pitch.　　100-C

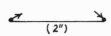

A rapid gliss up 1/4 tone for the indicated time, then return to original intonation.　　121

A rapid gliss to 1/4 tone higher or lower, with the sound fading away.　　121

A. A 1/4 tone gliss.
B. A 1/2 tone gliss.
C. A 3/4 tone gliss.　　105-A

Glissandi: 1/4 Tone (cont'd):

      A rapid bending of the pitch up 1/4
                          tone for each small arrow.   70-A

      A raising or lowering of the pitch of
                          the lower note so it beats against the
                          upper pitch. The numbers above the
                          sign indicate the number of beats that
                          are to be produced.   130-E

      A. A tone going flat.
                          B. A trailing-off gliss.   78; 86-B

   Very short, small glissandi in the in-
                          dicated direction.   52-C, 17

Glissandi (cont'd):

  Special Effects

   A downward gliss performed with a loud
                          crescendo.   105-A

      A wide vibrato-like gliss of a 1/4
                          tone span up and down.   4

      A gliss plus a semitone trill.   105-A

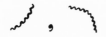   A glissando tremolo.   97-A

Glissandi: Special Effects (cont'd):

A gliss in the indicated direction
with tremolos.   10-A

A gliss plus a tremolo.   105-A

While the instrumentalist plays the
pitch shown by the regular notehead,
he sings the gliss shown by the 'X'
noteheads.   57-C

A short portamento-like gliss that
starts just before the next note.
(Duration is similar to a grace note.) 101-H

A gliss by all seven violins that follows the indicated contour. Note that
each violin starts on a separate pitch:
VN. 1 on pitch 1, VN. 2 on pitch 2, etc. 89-D

XXXXXX

A succession of glissandi played as
fast as possible.   96-B

A rapid nonchromatic gliss that trails
after the initial pitch is attacked.   51-D

HOLDS AND PAUSES

Various systems of holds and pauses are illustrated by the symbols below.

ʕ 9+ 9 ⸜	A. Prolonged (breathing) pause. 48
	B. Slightly prolonged pause. 93
	C. Short pause. 72-A, 65, 94-B
	D. Very short pause. 72-A, 54, 56, 48

⅄ ⅄	A. Short pause.
	B. Very short pause. 76

ℯ	Short pause. 59-A

,, [9]	A. Slightly prolonged pause.
	B. Very short pause. 13; 68

V VV VVV	A. A short pause
	B. Twice as long as a short pause.
	C. Three times as long as a short pause. 85

▼ ▼▼ ▼▼▼	Prolonged forms of A, B, and C above. 85

⅁ V ⌐	A. Short pause at the beginning of the phrase or unit.
	B. Short pause at the middle.
	C. Short pause at the end. 2-B

⅂⅁ W	A pause twice as long as above.
	A. Pause at the beginning.
	B. Pause at the end. 72-A

Any of the forms in the following eight lines may be made exact by adding a sign, either in beats or seconds, above the hold that most closely approximates the desired duration.

    A. Short hold (1.5-2 seconds).
    B. Medium hold (ca. 4 seconds).
    C. Long hold (5-6 seconds).
    D. Very long hold (10-15 seconds).

⋀ ⌢· ⸢·⸣ ⸢ᴏ⸣	57-C, 101-C
⋀ ⌢· ⸢·⸣ ⸢·⸜	37-B
⋀ ⌢· ⸢·⸣ ⸤·⸥	19-C
⸢·⸣	32-B
⊓	97-A, 19-B

Holds and Pauses (cont'd):

⊡ ⊟ ⊏⊟⊐   76

⌒• ⊡ ⌒⊡   85

⋏ ⊡ ⌒•   48

⋏ ⬦• ⊡ ⊡ ⌒• ⊙ ⊙⋏

A. About one second long.
B. About two seconds long.
C. About three seconds long.
D. About four seconds long.
E. About five seconds long.
F. About six seconds long.
G. About six plus one second long.   51-C

$\overset{5''}{\smile}$, $\overset{2''}{\smile}$, ⌒•(= ± ♩)   Hold for the number of seconds or beats
indicated. The plus/minus signs in-
dicate an approximation.   10-F; 23-C; 72-B

$\underset{3''}{\overset{⌒•}{}}$, ⊡ (±7'')   7-A; 72-B

$\overset{2}{\smile}$ Hold for two impulses at whatever tempo
the basic impulse may be.   44

$\overset{n}{3},$ $\overset{n}{n},$ A. Lengthen the pause in proportion to
the size of the number.
B. Length of the pause is left to the
performer.   94-B

$\overset{⌒}{V}$ A variable pause that is dependent on
one of the other parts.   93

⌒•———   Hold the tone for the appropriate duration, then continue the tone.   76

⬦   The two notes are connected by a fer-
mata and are to be held the appropriate
duration.   51-B

⋏ , ⸴   A. A short pause or cut.
B. A longer pause.   19-B

⌒•   Each performer is to continue the hold
for as long as possible; that is, until
the end of a breath or a bow, etc.   2-A

*hold for as long
as possible*

METRIC SIGNS

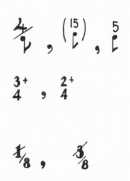

The numeral indicates the number of beats/unit. The note shows what type of note gets a beat.   63; 31-A, 87; 91-B

The plus sign shows that the unit has the indicated number of beats plus a partial beat.   50-A

These metric signs give the number of **1/8** notes/measure. The slash mark indicates that these eighth notes are grace notes.   15-B

This sign replaces the regular meter sign and signifies no meter or a free meter.   94-A

Metric Signs (cont'd):

Subdivisions of Units

The top numbers indicate the grouping of the beats.   34-B, 51-E
  A. Two beats plus three beats.
  B. Two plus two beats plus one beat.

A seven-beat measure divided into two plus two plus three beats.   91-C

A five-beat measure divided into two beats plus three beats.   49-A

A seven-beat measure divided into two plus three plus two beats. Note that two beams are used for meters that are based on 16th notes.   49-A

A. Division into two plus three beats.
B. Division into three plus four beats.
    71-D, 2-D; 15-A, 70-B, 95

A. Division into one plus two beats.
B. Division into a double-two plus a
   double-four grouping.   71-D

A division into six plus six beats is notated by doubling the sign for three beats, or writing the desired number into a related sign.   72-A, 75; 71-D

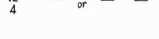

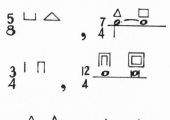

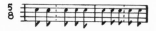

The dotted line indicates the grouping of the beats.   102, 34-A, 12-B

MELODIC LINE

Melodic line: A. Primary.   22-D

                 B. Secondary.   22-D

                 C. Tertiary.   22-D

Principal melodic line (Hauptstimme). 107-A

Secondary melodic line (Nebenstimme). 107-A

The dotted line indicates the direction of the melodic lines that go from one performer to another.   34-A

The line shows the order of the pitches for each part.   108

The brackets indicate the phrase groupings.   30

Follow the dotted line from the first note, either up or down.   86-D

Play the indicated pitches as fast as possible, starting from any pitch.   37-B

All the figures within the box are to be played; the starting point is to be determined by the conductor or the performer.   15-C

The group may be read from any point and in any direction. It is to be played as fast as possible and continued; or, if interrupted, a note must be held until the end of the horizontal line.   10-G

Melodic Line (cont'd):

The group is to be read from any point
going either left or right. Always
playing as fast as possible, the performer is to vary as much as possible
and continue until the end of the rectangle.   96-D

The performer starts from the left and
plays all the notes there is time for. 42-A

The arrow indicates that the parts
that were divisi are now written on
the same staff.   80-B

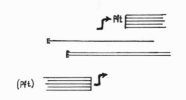

The bent arrow indicates that the
piano part has been changed to another
staff.   15-B

The arrow indicates that the held notes
are still to be held, but are written
on a different staff.   23-D

MORDENTS

A. A mordent up to the next note.
B. A mordent down to the next note.   23-D

Mordent to a tone that is 1/4 tone
higher.   121

OCTAVE SIGNS

𝄞 𝄢	A. One octave higher. B. One octave lower.	119-C
𝄞 𝄢		96-D
8↑ 8↓		23-C, 101-C
+8--- -8---		85
𝄞 𝄞		23-B
8 8		21-B
|5↑ |5↓	A. Two octaves higher. B. Two octaves lower.	23-C
2 Okt--- 𝄢		51-D; 115

	The whole chord is to be played one octave higher.	2-B
8va Bassa	Only the notes under the dotted line are to be played one octave lower.	101-C
8 bassa	The circled pitches are to be played one octave lower.	109

PERCUSSIVE EFFECTS

Applaud (clap) for the duration of the half-note written above the staff.   10-D

A. Clap hands.
B. Fast clapping for the duration of the horizontal line.   96-B

Snapping of fingers.   96-B; 51-C; 45

Gentle snapping of fingers.   10-A

Rub the feet on the floor in a circular manner.   97-A

Strike heel on the floor.   9

Lightly tap foot on the floor to the indicated rhythm.   58

African tongue click combined with finger-snapping.   25-A

A tongue click in the register of the accompanying pitch.   116-E

Make a noise.   57-D

REPEATS

Repeat the pitch once for each stem. 89-B

Repeat the whole chord to the rhythm indicated at the top of the staff. 47-C

The chord is to be repeated to the rhythm of the empty stems. 111-A

The slash-marks indicate a repeat of the pitch for each mark and in the rhythm of the spacing shown. 5

Repeat the chord once for each slash-mark in the rhythm indicated by the spacing. 67-A

Repeat the same note. 111-A

An extremely fast repeated note. 89-B, 116-A

Repeat the note rapidly. 90-C

Repeat the tone as rapidly as possible. 59-A

Repeats (cont'd):

Aperiodic

Rapid aperiodic repetitions of the tone. 111-A

Aperiodic succession of notes. 111-A

Repeats (cont'd):

Groups and Phrases

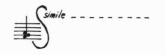 Repeat the group of notes.   111-A, 89-B

 Repeat the whole group until the end
of the broken line.   105-E

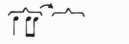 The group of notes is to be repeated
for the duration of each bracket,
but in the rhythm of the spacing of
the brackets.   105-D

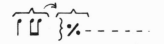 Repeat the figure under the first
bracket.   57-A

 Continue to repeat the figure under
the bracket for the duration of the
broken line.   57-A

 Repeat the group of notes until the
end of the horizontal line.   69-A

VN
 Repeat over and over until the other
performers have finished their material.   10-F
VA

 Repeat until the end of the arrow.   104-B

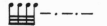 Repeat the phrase until a sign from the
conductor denotes the end of the
structure.   49-B

 Repeat the phrase as quickly as possi-
ble until the sign to which the arrow
points is reached.   49-B

Repeats: Groups and Phrases (cont'd):

Keep repeating the material until a
sign to stop is given.   48

Continue playing the indicated notes
as fast as possible.   96-C

Continue repeating the notes until the
end of the horizontal lines.   91-B

Repeats (cont'd):

Continuing Patterns

Continue the pattern upward until the
end of the arrow.   10-G

Continue the pattern until the end of
the wavy line.   12-A, 46

23-B

Continue the pattern upward following
the limits shown.   105-B

Continue the group or configuration.   98

Repeat the group. Use the top slurs
for the first time through and the
bottom slurs for the second.   28

First, phrase the material according
to the top brackets, then according
to the bottom brackets.   48

RHYTHM

Strict

Play the material in strict rhythm.   62-A

Maintain strict rhythm without any
sort of accentuation.   49-C

The first note of the group is to be
played as a downbeat.   125

The forked stem indicates notes of a
cluster, not an arpeggiated chord.   101-H

Indicates four double-stops that are
to be attacked and played together by
violins 1-4.   59-B

(7:2″)

Indicates that seven equal notes are
to be played in two seconds.   119-C

⌐5p4¬ , ⌐5:6¬

A. Five notes in the time of four.
B. Five notes in the time of six.   2-D; 70-B

⌐4a3¬ , ⌐5pour6¬

A. Four notes in the time of three.
B. Five notes in the time of six. 23-D; 15-D

⌐7(8)¬ , 7♪=♩

A. Seven notes in the time of eight.
B. Seven 16th notes in one quarter-
   note.   10-B; 22-A, 79

Rhythm: Strict (cont'd):

Ten attacks in the span of a quarter-
note.   122-B, 22-A

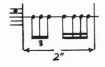

A. Single attack.
B. Double attack.
C. Triple attack.   38

Triple attack (quasi triplet).   57-C

Play the pitch indicated on the five-
line staff to the rhythm shown on the
single line.   88

An example in which the beaming extends over the rest.   101-G, 111-E

Since the notes are widely separated,
the rests are placed between the
beaming.   12-B

The dotted line indicates that the
rest refers to the eighth-note.   2-D

The eighth-note is the basic impulse.
The dotted line is used to indicate
the unarticulated impulses.   51-F

Each player is to enter according to
his number. Player one first, player
two second, etc.   67-A

Rhythm (cont'd):

Free

     or

Within the given sections, the rhythmic values need not be strictly observed.   89-C, 62-A

In sections where black and red notations appear together, red notation indicates exact rhythm and black notation freer rhythm. (In this example, small arrows indicate the red notes.)   34-D

The jagged line indicates what notes are to be played, and the spacing indicates the rhythm.   80-A

The indicated section is to be played in a free manner.   15-B

The plain noteheads indicate free rhythm and tempo.   83

The noteheads indicate attacks and the rhythm is shown by the spacing of the notes.   90-A

$$\left[\;\rule{0pt}{1em}\right]$$

Free rhythm within one breath.   49-B

SIGNALS

Conductor

m.d.   *m.g.*

r.h.   **l.h.**

A. Right hand.
B. Left hand.   15-C

5   2
① ②③   ④⑤ ①   ②

The large numerals show the number of
impulses in the unit; the small numerals show where they are to occur
in the unit.   2-A

2 s   *3 s*

2 signes   *3 signes*

The numerals show the number of impulses in each unit. ('S' = signes)   15-B

2   3

↑   ↑   ↑   ↑ ↑

The numerals indicate the number of
impulses in the unit; the arrows show
where they occur.   15-B

m.d. *1.*———*2.*———*3.*—*4.*——↕

The numerals indicate the number of
right-hand beats; the line shows the
duration of each beat.   15-C

[*3 signes*]   1   2   3

A unit of three impulses; the arrows
indicate when the impulses occur.   2-A

↓

A downward gesture.

→

A gesture to the right.

↖

An upward gesture.   10-G

↓   ← → ↖

The hand positions in beating a 4/4
measure or 4/impulse unit.   2-A

↓   → ↖

Hand positions in a 3/4 or 3/impulse
time unit.   2-A

↓ ↓ ← → ↖

Hand positions in a 5/4 or 5/impulse
time unit.   2-A

Signals: Conductor (cont'd):

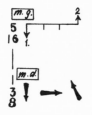

The top sign shows the position of the left-hand impulses that are grouped into three plus two. The bottom sign shows the three impulses of the right hand and their positions.   2-A

The large arrows indicate beginnings of groups, and small arrows show the impulses in the groups. A change of speed is shown by change of arrow color. The speed of the impulses is shown in metronome marks (M.M.).   8

The downward arrows indicate precise moments, while the upward arrow is like an upbeat and is not to be precise.   72-A

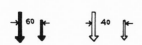

The right hand beats subunits of the left-hand beats. The order of the beats is free; their durations are indicated in beats, by the numbers in the box.   15-C

The numbers refer to the durations of the time units. When two numbers are superimposed, the conductor is free to choose either one.   15-C

A. A downbeat.
B. A beat that may be omitted.
                              7-B, 24-A, 10-F; 48

Signals (cont'd):

Performer

   A. An accent or beat.
B. An upbeat or afterbeat.   34-E; 42-C; 34-E

   These signals indicate the beats and
/or the order of entrances in the
performers' parts.   2-A, 96-B

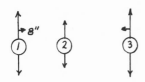   Signals from the conductor are aligned
with events by the use of arrows. They
help the performer place the entrances
of events.   56

   Entrances from the conductor cueing
the performers' attacks and cut-offs.   49-B

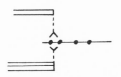   The Y-shaped line (人) is used to in-
dicate an approximate alignment of the
event.   51-E

   A. The broken-line arrow indicates an
approximate alignment of events.
B. The solid-line arrow indicates precise, simultaneous attacks. 7-B; 7-B, 22-A

   A system of cueing that is written in
the center of the score and shows the
order of events. Since more than one
performer may be involved, this cue-
ing shows the composite sound of all
performers.   51-E

TREMOLOS

Even Rhythm

A. A slow tremolo.
B. A normal tremolo.
C. A fast tremolo.   6-B

A tremolo that has ten articulations
in the span of a quarter-note.   22-B

A tremolo between the indicated
pitches. (Note that the difference
between a tremolo and a trill has to
do with the interval of the tremolo;
an interval larger than an augmented
2nd is called a tremolo, while an interval of an augmented 2nd or smaller
is a trill.)   96-E; 103, 57-C

23-B; 51-D

Tremolo between the indicated notes
until the end of the jagged line.
                             19-B; 119-B, 10-F

A. Tremolo until the end of the curly
   line.   16-B
B. Tremolo between the indicated notes. 111-B

A. Tremolo.   78, 24-B, 111-C
B. Flutter-tongue for the duration of
   the horizontal line.   90-C

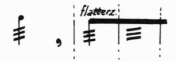

Tremolo for the duration of the dotted
line.   16-A

Continue the tremolo through all the
measures with the slurs and the slash-
marks.   15-B

Tremolos: Even Rhythm (cont'd):

Tremolo at the approximate pitch indicated by the stem. The dotted line
indicates that the tremolo gradually
fades away.   10-D

A tremolo that retards in accordance
with the slash-marks.   5

A tremolo that slows down in accordance with the lengthening of the
wavy line.   80-B, 101-D, E, 12-C

A tremolo, between the two pitches,
that is to speed up in accordance
with the shortening excursion of the
wavy line.   111-A

Tremolos (cont'd):

  Arhythmic

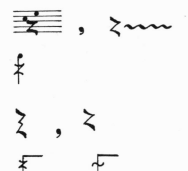

An uneven tremolo between the indicated
pitches.   111-B; 80-A, 89-C, 59-B

                                          111-C, 47-B

A. A fast uneven tremolo.   47-B
B. An uneven tremolo of normal speed.   47-B

                                          67-A

Tremolos (cont'd):

  Glissandi

Tremolo glissandi.
    A. Slow tremolo gliss.
    B. Normal-speed tremolo gliss.
    C. Fast tremolo gliss.   105-A

A glissando tremolo.   93

TRILLS

A trill that goes up to the natural
note above the written note.   26

A trill that goes to the small note.
                        91-G, 66, 99, 10-F

Trill between the indicated notes.   86-A

A. A normal trill until the end of the
   wavy line.
B. A normal trill that speeds up in
   relation to the wavy line.   111-A

Trill until the end of the wavy line.   97-A, 45
   A. Fast trill.
   B. Slow trill.

A. A trill to the next note up.
B. A trill to the next note down.   85

Trill either up or down.   38

A trill within a semitone.   14-B

A trill within a whole tone.   14-B

A. Trill 1/4 tone up.
B. Trill 1/4 tone down.   113-C

Trills (cont'd):

Rapidly trill to both upper notes
(double trill).   89-A

                                                       53

Play the indicated notes rapidly and
legato, like a widened trill.   111-A

                                                       35

A trill whose interval gets wider ac-
cording to the width of the wavy line.   85

A trill that slows down at the arrow.   72-A

A trill that speeds up at the arrow.   72-A

A. Trill as fast as possible to the
   end of the bracket.
B. Hold the trill as long as possible.   27

The notes that follow the trill are to
be played at the same speed as the
trill.   12-C

VIBRATO

Symbol	Description	Reference
NV , SV , S	A. Non vibrato. B. and C. Senza vibrato.	129, 23-C, 86-D 24-B; 24-B
ᴡᴠ_____	Without vibrato until the end of the line.	101-H
N , v , ∾	Normal vibrato.	100-A; 24-B, 129; 21-C
⌐∿∿ , ⌐ʌʌʌʌ	Normal vibrato.	69; 6-A
v.l. , ∨‒∿‒	Slow vibrato (vibrato lento).	44; 73
⌐∿∿∿ , ⌐ʌʌʌʌ		69; 6-A
VR , SV , ∨∿∿∿	A. Rapid vibrato. B. Stressed vibrato. C. Vibrato presto.	44 100-A 73
∿∿∿ , ʌʌʌʌ	Fast vibrato.	59-B, 89-B; 6-A
♪ , ‒∿∿ , ʌʌ∿∿	Begin the vibrato fast, then decrease the speed of the vibrato.	90-B; 52-C, 9; 6-A
o‒ ‒ ‒ ➤ vib. molto ‒ ‒ ➤ non vib.	Go from normal vibrato to fast vibrato to non vibrato.	36
o(♮♮)∿∿ , ↕∿∿	A vibrato that goes up and down 1/4 tone.	28; 89-E
∿∿∿∿∿	A wide and slow vibrato that fluctuates up to a 1/2 step.	25-A

PLACEMENT OF EVENTS

The sign indicates that the conductor has a choice of the top event or the bottom event.

15-C

Indicates a choice of musical events; the choice is left to the discretion of the conductor.

37-B

When two sets of indications are super-imposed, choose either all the top or all the bottom indications.

37-B

Use a random aperiodic assortment of the indicated signs.

42-D

The indicated material is to be played in any order.

37-B

A sustained sound held to the end of the given over-all duration.

A sustained sound to be played any time in the over-all duration.

A short sound played any time within the over-all duration.

39

The group of notes is to be freely placed within the duration indicated by the bracketed 1/2 note.

37-A

Place the material, under the bracket, freely within the duration of the square note.

2-A

Placement of Events (cont'd):

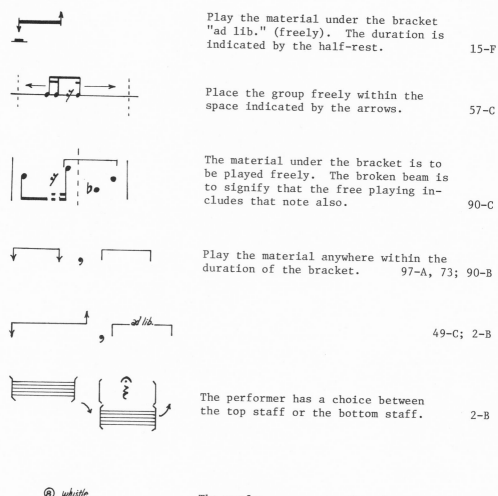

Play the material under the bracket
"ad lib." (freely). The duration is
indicated by the half-rest.   15-F

Place the group freely within the
space indicated by the arrows.   57-C

The material under the bracket is to
be played freely. The broken beam is
to signify that the free playing in-
cludes that note also.   90-C

Play the material anywhere within the
duration of the bracket.   97-A, 73; 90-B

                                         49-C; 2-B

The performer has a choice between
the top staff or the bottom staff.   2-B

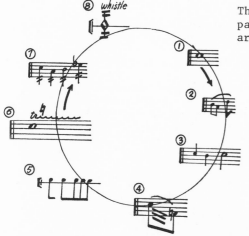

The performers are to play these
passages in the order in which they
are numbered.   31-A

FREE VARIATION AND IMPROVISATION

Repeat and vary the chords or notes
under the sign.   4

Repeat the pitches while varying the
durations.   47-A

Repeat "ad libitum" (freely) the in-
dicated pitches.   119-A

Improvise, maintaining at least one of
the preceding paramaters.   11

The phrase is to be played once rather
fast; then it is to be repeated in
fragments from any point.   42-D

A free section in which the performer
is to play "ad lib." using some or all
the available time until the next
event.   100-E

Play freely the material within the
box for the duration indicated above
the box.   97-A

Free Variation and Improvisation (cont'd):

The performer is to distribute the notes or groups of notes and dynamics freely within the limits shown by the space of the box.

           51-B, 89-B, 10-G, 121, 15-C, 96-D

           96-E

A random playing of the patterns within the box.   35, 42-D

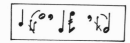

Play freely in any order.   86-D

Improvise on these notes, maintaining a rather thick texture.   10-H

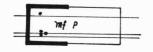

Improvise on these notes, but go from a thick texture to a thin texture.   10-H

Improvise on these notes, but gradually go from a thick texture to a thin texture.   10-H

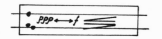

Improvise on the given notes, going freely from the 'ppp' to the 'f' dynamic.   10-H

Free Variation and Improvisation (cont'd):

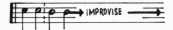

Improvise until the end of the arrow.   34-C

Play the notes in any order without repeating the same note twice in succession. Apply the signs in the boxes to the pitches without using the same sign twice in a row.   7-B

Play the given note, changing freely its manner of realization: either play it flutter-tonguing, duration of each note 0.1-0.5"; or repeat the note in groups from one to five notes.   119-B

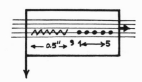

lento

Play the material under the broken lines slowly (outside the regular tempo).   51-E

Improvise freely on the given notes, using them in any order.   34-C

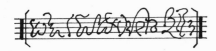

Improvise freely over the entire range of the instrument.   41

STRINGS

CHAPTER II. STRINGS

ARPEGGIOS

Arco and Pizzicato

 ,   A. Arpeggio upward.
B. Arpeggio downward.   57-C

  Arpeggio in any direction.   57-B

  Strum across the strings in the direc-
tion indicated.   45

Arpeggiate pizzicato the notes in the
indicated direction.   110

 The chord is repeated four times (once
for each vertical line); the direction
of the arpeggio is changed each time.   105-D

BOWING

Arco

ar. , ord. , or. , ARCO   Play with the bow in the normal, ordinary manner.   59-B; 89-E; 59-B; 57-B

A , N, AN   25-B; 84-C; 111-A, 130-F

V   n
ʃ , ʃ   A. Up bow.
              B. Down bow.   82

⊓⊓⊓ , VVV   A number of quick bowings in the in-
              dicated direction, always irregular.   89-B

Bowing: Arco (cont'd):

⊓ V   Several irregular bow strokes up and
                                       down in succession.   89-D

⊓V , V⊓   Several changes of bow strokes accord-
                                       ing to the dynamics.   59-B

↰↲   Changes in the direction of the bow.   9

⎢⎢⎢⎢   Bow at the heel of the bow: use exces-
                                       sive pressure so that the string creaks
                                       and jars.   89-D

⩔⊓ , ⊓   Excessive pressure on the string with
                                       the bow in the indicated direction.
                                                                    57-B, 28; 98

⌿♩   Choke the string by excessively hard
                                       and slow bowing.   35

gradually to
normal pressure   Excessive bow pressure changing gradu-
b∿∿∿∿∿_____   ally to normal pressure.   31-A

⊙⌒_____   To be played on one bowing from tip
                                       to frog.   10-F

⌐   ¬   Entire bow.   19-C

[Upper half of bow.   19-C

]   Lower half of bow.   19-C

⌐¬   Heel of the bow.   19-C

V , a.p.   Point or tip of the bow.   19-C, 45; 121

Bowing: Arco (cont'd):

punta _ _ _ _ _ _ | Play on the tip of the bow for the duration of the broken line. | 51-E

Strike the strings with the bow in the middle of the fingerboard. 97-B

X | Strike with the bow, not necessarily with the wood. | 29

Strike the strings with the bow. 119-C

Drag the heel of the bow across the strings while fingering pitches synchronously. 45

FINGER | Draw the bow or strike with the bow near the point where the finger(s) are stopping the string. | 57-B

AFL | Bow as though playing harmonics. | 111-C

Bowing (cont'd):

Col legno

LT , AL , L , cl | Bow with the wood of the bow. 57-B; 53; 128-C, 61; 86-D

L S. | 19-C

| 45

, | A. Bow with the wood of the bow. B. Cease bowing with the wood. | 9

, | A. Bow with the wood of the bow. B. Cease bowing with the wood. | 6-B

Bowing (cont'd):

Battuto col legno

LB , *c.l.b.* , **X** , *f. cl.*   Strike with the wood of the bow.
                                     111-C, 57-B; 25-B, 84-G; 59-B; 130-F

l. batt. , ⌒ , ℟   89-D; 24-B; 130-A

Symbol	Description	Ref
	A. Strike or bounce with the wood of the bow.	
	B. Cease striking or bouncing.	9
	A. Strike with the wood of the bow.	
	B. Cease striking.	6-B
+	Strike with the wood of the bow.	80-A
	Press all the strings against the fingerboard at any point, and strike them with the wood of the bow.	80-A
	Strike with the wood of the bow according to the number and spacing of the slash (‖‖) marks.	130-D
	Stop the strings anywhere along the fingerboard, and strike the strings in front of the bridge with the wood of the bow.	80-B
	With the wood of the bow, strike the top of the bridge.	80-B
	Strike with the wood of the bow between the bridge and tailpiece.	80-A
	Strike the strings with the wood of the bow in the middle of the fingerboard.	97-A
1/2 LT , *Ag.* , **ANM**	Play with the hair and wood of the bow simultaneously. 57-B; 25-B; 111-C	
APM	Play with the hair and wood of the bow simultaneously near the bridge. 111-C	

Bowing (cont'd):

Near the Bridge (sul ponticello)

PONT , P , a.s.p. , a.S.   Near the bridge.   57-B; 24-B; 130-F; 16-B

Pt. , vp , SP, AP   128-C; 25-C, 19-C; 86-D, 45; 111-A

∩   35, 10-F

▬   Play on the side of the bridge. ("On the side" means near the bridge.)   61

▲ , ⌂   A. Play near the bridge.
B. Cease playing near the bridge.   9, 6-B

Bowing (cont'd):

On the Bridge (ponticello)

PONT , L, ↑   Play on the bridge.   57-B; 121; 89-E

♯ , ▬   A. Strike on the bridge.
B. Bow on the bridge.   61

▲ , ⌂   A. Play on the bridge.
B. Cease playing on the bridge.   9

   Play on the bridge on the indicated strings.   25-B

Bowing: On the Bridge (ponticello) (cont'd):

	Play on the bridge, or press against the mute when the mute is on. 10-F
	Exaggerated ponticello, or press against the mute (more harmonics are produced than normally) so the pitch is almost totally obscured. 35
	Play by bouncing the bow at the frog across the bridge. 10-F
	Strongly press the bow on the bridge. 54
	Play directly on the bridge. 7-A
	Heel of the bow on the bridge. 45
	Play on the bridge perpendicular to the right-hand edge. 89-D
	Bow on the bridge with the wood of the bow. 124
	A. Strike with the heel on the bridge. B. Cease striking. 6-B

Bowing (cont'd):

Behind the Bridge

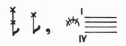   Play behind the bridge (between bridge
                       and tailpiece) on the indicated string.
                                              121, 71-C; 57-B

   4; 25-B

   Play between the bridge and tailpiece
                       on the indicated string.   89-D; 90-B; 119-B

   Play between the bridge and tailpiece.
                            76; 32-B; 59-B, 9, 111-B; 14-B; 97-A

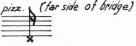   Arpeggiate (on the four strings) be-
                       tween the bridge and tailpiece in the
                       direction indicated. 59-B, 19-A; 89-D; 89-C

                                              104-B; 31-A

                       Play between the bridge and tailpiece.   78

   Pizzicato between the bridge and tail-
                       piece on the indicated string.   12-B

                                              104-B

   A rapid, irregular tremolo played be-
                       tween the bridge and tailpiece on the
                       indicated string.   104-B

                       Play between the bridge and tailpiece
                       with the hair and wood of bow simul-
                       taneously (percussive effect).   25-B

Bowing (cont'd):

Saltando

3   2   2

Bounce the tip of the bow along the
length of a specified string while the
fingers damp the strings. (Numbers beneath the symbols represent relative
durational values. Player chooses
basic unit value.)   94-A

Ricochet; bounce the bow freely on the
string (p), or stretch the hair of the
bow by pressing it at the nut with the
thumb (mf-f).   119-B

 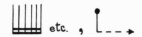, **ric**.

Ricochet; let the bow bounce on the
string.   89-A; 89-B

  etc. ,

105-A; 119-C

Ricochet the wood of the bow on the
strings while the left hand lightly
stops the strings to prevent distinct
pitches. The only pitch heard is produced by the strings between the bridge
and the bow. The pitch descends as the
bow moves away from the bridge.   35

Bounce the wood of the bow on the
strings.   45

Freely bounce the wood of the bow along
the lengths of the specified strings
while the fingers lightly damp the
strings near the nut. The direction
of the bow is indicated.   94-A

Same as above, except that the bow
crosses over to the indicated strings
at the middle of the fingerboard.   94-A

Spiccato: detached or bouncing bow.   29

Bowing (cont'd):

   Sul tasto (over the fingerboard)

T , t , ST , AT , *tasto--¬*   Play over the fingerboard.
                                      19-C; 24-B; 86-D; 111-C; 51-E

      ▼ , ▽   A. Play over the fingerboard.
                    B. Cease playing over the fingerboard. 6-B

      ▼ , ▽   A. Play over fingerboard near the stop-
                       ping fingers or nut.
                    B. Cease playing in this manner.   9

Bowing (cont'd):

   On the Tailpiece

     ┼ , ↑ , ▤   Bow on the tailpiece.   124; 14-A; 119-B

     ▼   Play over the tailpiece. Strike with
                the bow.   61

     ▼—   Play on the upper part of the tailpiece. 61

     ▼—   Play on the lower part of the tailpiece. 61

     TP   Play with the heel of the bow on the
                tailpiece.   45

     ☼   Tap the tailpiece with the bow stick. 25-B

Bowing (cont'd):

   Between the Pegs and the Fingerboard

     Ш , ╫—   Play on the strings between the pegs
                  and the fingerboard.   25-B; 61

Bowing (cont'd):

From One Position to Another

T____ ....Ω   A gradual change of bowing from over
                                  the fingerboard to near the bridge.   10-F

tasto ⟶ *pont.*   84-B

tasto ---- *⟋ord.* *⟋pont.*   A change of bowing from over the
                                  fingerboard to normal bowing to bowing
                                  near the bridge.   51-E

tasto ⇄ *ord.* ⇄ *pont.*   Constantly change the bowing between
                                  the indicated areas: over the finger-
                                  board, normal bowing, and near the
                                  bridge.   51-E

- - - - - ⟶ pont.   A gradual change of bowing from ordi-
                                  nary bowing to bowing near the bridge.   36

s.p. ⟶ *ord.* ⟶ *s.p.*   A change of bowing from near the bridge
                                  to ordinary to near the bridge.   89-F

Ω____ ....*ORD.*   A gradual change of bowing from the
                                  frog across the bridge to ordinary
                                  bowing.   10-F

Ω ____ ....T_   A gradual change in bowing from over
                                  the bridge to over the fingerboard.   10-F

                                  Bow with the wood of the bow from near
                                  the bridge to over the fingerboard.   45

ord. ⟶ *tasto* *⟋ord.*   A change of bowing from ordinary to
                                  over the fingerboard to ordinary.   51-E

ARCO   Strike or pluck between the bow and
  ↑   the bridge. Draw the bow at the point
  ↓   of the given pitch and press. (Cellos
PONT   and basses only.)   57-B

                                  Produce changes of:
                                     A. Timbre by an action other than
                                        changing fingering; e.g., bow
I   ⊢━━━┤   pressure, pizz., change of string.
                                     B. Pitch by a change in fingering
                                        while maintaining a continuous
                                        action (bowing, pizz., etc.).   128-A

DAMP

Damp immediately.   89-E

Damp.   15-B

Damp string either with next finger of
left hand, or release and damp lightly
with stopping finger.   35

GLISSANDI

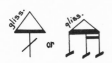

Two instruments that glissando to the
same note.   15-A

A double-stop with the lower note
glissando in the indicated direction.
The rhythm applies to both notes.   71-A

A double-stop glissando.   130-D

Strike the strings with the wood of
the bow; with the left hand stop all
the strings and glissando toward the
bridge.   80-B

Glissando over several strings in the
indicated direction.   57-D

Glissando over the strings in imitation
of the line pattern indicated.   3

Glissandi (cont'd):

A very slight glissando from one har-
monic to the next.   15-A

Tremolo the indicated harmonics while
making a glissando.   71-E

A pizzicato glissando in which the
glissando occurs after the note has
sounded for a short time.   7-A

A pizzicato glissando.   78

A finger glissando during which a percussive bounce of the bow occurs on the
same string.   45

Finger glissando, then add the bow.   45

A finger glissando during which the bow
is added and then taken away. The
glissando continues.   45

Strike the string with the finger, and
glissando in the indicated direction.   61

A downward glissando on an open string
by turning the tuning peg.   89-F

A glissando pizzicato by turning the
tuning peg.   105-A

Glissandi (cont'd):

Tremolos

The finger of the left hand glissandos in the normal manner, while the first two fingers of the right hand pluck or tremolo the same string on both sides of the left-hand finger. 45

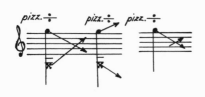

The same as above, except that the "X" indicates which string is to be used.
  A. LH glisses downward.
  B. LH glisses upward.
  C. Choice of string ad lib. 101-H

The same as above, except that the right hand tremolos while the left hand glissandos downward. 101-H

A tremolo glissando that ends on the last thirty-second note before the next beat. 71-B

A tremolo glissando. 99

A tremolo glissando: speed is proportional to the number of slashes. 105-A

A tremolo glissando. 105-A

Glissandi (cont'd):

Along the String

Movement ("glissando") along the string. 57-D

Slide the bow toward the bridge of the instrument. 7-B

HARMONICS

O , O→ , O—   Harmonics.   21-C, 19-C; 101-A; 45

Harmonic stop.   57-B

Place finger lightly on the string.
                                               19-C, 24-B

A harmonic stop without the fundamental tone being given. (Use third,
fourth, fifth, sixth harmonic, etc.,
ad lib.)   57-B

1/2 harmonic stop: the finger touches
the string a bit more firmly than for
a normal harmonic. The fundamental
tone is ad libitum.   57-B

(N) o (N) o   Combine normal sounds (N) with harmonic
                                        sounds.   89-A

A pulled harmonic, wavering in pitch.   45

△   Highest possible harmonic (indefinite
                                        pitch).   25-B

The note in parentheses is the sound
realized from the harmonic stop and
is read in the small treble clef.   84-G

Harmonics with different timbres.   6-B

HIGHEST PITCH POSSIBLE

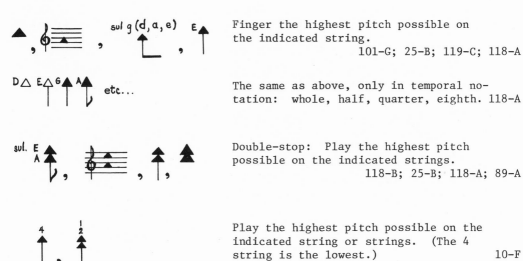

Finger the highest pitch possible on the indicated string.
101-G; 25-B; 119-C; 118-A

The same as above, only in temporal notation: whole, half, quarter, eighth. 118-A

Double-stop: Play the highest pitch possible on the indicated strings.
118-B; 25-B; 118-A; 89-A

Play the highest pitch possible on the indicated string or strings. (The 4 string is the lowest.) 10-F

Play in quick succession the highest note possible on each of the indicated strings. 10-F

Play very high notes on the indicated strings. The length of the stems indicates the relative pitch. (The taller the stem, the higher the pitch.) 10-F

MUTING

S.S. , C.S.

Without mute; with mute. 59-B; 89-B

⊔⊔ , ⊓⊓

19-C, 25-B, 15-B

35, 10-F

9, 6-B

(via sord.) , +

121; 64

A. With mute when playing horizontally.
B. With mute when playing vertically.
C. Without mute.
(These signs refer to 'mobiles,' where horizontally means reading across the page, and vertically, reading down the page.) 51-C

OVERBOWING EFFECTS

Produce a noise by overbowing the four
strings. The pitches are not important.   54

Broken sound produced by overbowing.   6-B

Bowing with too much pressure in order
to produce a noise effect.   89-B

A scratch tone: pitch unimportant.   32-B

Scratch the string with the hair of
the bow.   9

"Scratching" effect.   61

Transition from "scratching" to
normal tone production.   61

Transition from normal tone production
to "scratching."   61

Scrape with the fingernail along the
lowest string in the indicated direction.   7-A

PIZZICATO

Pizzicato.   24-B; 59-B, 111-A; 73; 130-A

Pizzicato in the normal manner.   111-D

A. Pizzicato with one finger.
B. Pizzicato with two fingers.   119-C

Pizzicato (cont'd):

(, **(**	A. Pizzicato. B. Cease playing pizzicato.	6-B, 9
	Pluck the indicated string.	65
pizz.	Pluck both notes together.	31-B

(, **(** , **(** , **(**	Pizzicato:
	  A. Near the bridge.
	  B. Over the fingerboard.
	  C. Tremolo.
	  D. With the fingertip.
		6-B, 9

PzP	Pizzicato near the bridge.	111-C
Sul tasto — secco	Pluck very close to the finger stopping the string.	22-B
	Damp the string before plucking.	57-C
	Damp the string before plucking; play staccato.	57-C
pizz. *ffff*	A strong pizzicato so that the string rebounds against the fingerboard.	2-D; 28; 80-A; 19-C
		67-A; 4; 15-D; 78; 24-C
	A. Strong pizzicato, string striking the fingerboard. B. Weak pizzicato.	61 61, 29

Pizzicato (cont'd):

Pluck the string so that it rebounds
against the fingerboard.   9

The same as above, only raise the
finger slowly.   9

Pizzicato, immediately fading away.   9

Right-hand pizzicato while the left
hand presses lightly on the string
(wooden tone).   24-B

The note in brackets is to be stopped
in the normal manner, while the thumb
plays on the part of the string between the nut and the stopping finger.
The resulting sound is ♭♪ .   130-E

The "X" indicates the string on which
the note is to be fingered.
    A. Pluck the string on both sides
       of the stopping finger.
    B. Pluck string between nut and
       stopping finger.   101-H

Pizzicato (cont'd):

Left Hand

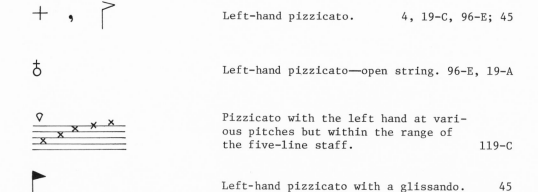

Left-hand pizzicato.   4, 19-C, 96-E; 45

Left-hand pizzicato—open string. 96-E, 19-A

Pizzicato with the left hand at various pitches but within the range of
the five-line staff.   119-C

Left-hand pizzicato with a glissando.   45

Pizzicato (cont'd):

Fingernail

⌒ , ▼ , ♪   Pizzicato with the fingernail.

19-B; 22-B; 31-A

🗲   Strike the string with a fingernail.   9

⊕   Pizzicato with the fingernail near the
bridge.   54

∪̆ , ∪   Pizzicato with the right hand, while
N   stopping the string with the fingernail of the left hand.   24-B; 24-C

①, ②, ③ *etc.*   Stop the note by pressing the fingernail vertically on the string, thus
producing a guitar-like sound. The
number indicates the stopping finger.   22-B

N♀   Stop the string with the tip of the
fingernail while bowing or striking
with the bow.   57-B

N⌐ , o—   Right-hand pizzicato while the left-
hand fingernail is next to or under
the string. A distorted, jangling
sound is produced.   57-B; 24-C

Pizzicato (cont'd):

Plectrum

▽ , ◊   Pizzicato with the plectrum.   73; 119-B

Pizzicato (cont'd):

Battuto (by striking)

♩ , PzB , ⊔ , ⊖   Strike the string with the fingertip of
the right hand.   28; 111-C; 121; 24-B

F—↯→   Slap the strings with the fingertips
of the left hand. (F = finger.)   57-B

near bridge
center
fingerboard

Strike the open strings with the
finger in the area indicated.   84-B

Pizzicato: Battuto (cont'd):

Tap on the strings with the fingers: "tapping tremolo."   28; 89-F

Stop the indicated note with a percussive effect of the left-hand finger. No use of right hand.   19-C; 24-C

Trill by tapping the string with a finger of the left hand only:
  A. Minor third trill.
  B. Major third trill.
  C. Minor second trill.   105-A

Strike the string with the fingertip between the bridge and the tailpiece.   14-B

Strike the strings with the palm of the hand.   59-A; 105-A; 9

Strike the open strings with the palm of the hand in the area of the fingerboard indicated.   25-D

Strike the strings with the open hand or fingers.   119-C; 73, 25-B; 28

Strike the strings with the open hand.   97-B

Strike the strings with the open hand in the notated range.   111-B

Strike the strings with the fingers.   24-C

Slap the fingers of the left hand on the fingerboard.   32-B

Strike the strings with the open hand on the fingerboard.   89-E

Produce noises on the indicated strings between the bridge and tailpiece.   119-C

STRIKE BODY OF INSTRUMENT

Tap the belly of the instrument with
the knuckles.   25-B; 61

Strike the back of the instrument
with the flat of the hand.   61

Play on the body of the instrument
between the bridge and fingerboard.   61

Strike the top of the instrument with
one finger.   61

Strike the top of the instrument with
four fingers.   61

With a fingertip, tap the front sec-
tion of the top of the instrument.   61

With a knuckle, tap the front section
of the top of the instrument.   61

In the middle section of the top of the
instrument (A) tap with finger, (B) tap
with knuckle.   61

At the rear section of the top of the
instrument (A) tap with finger, (B)
tap with knuckle.   61

Tap the body of the instrument. The
upper sign refers to the side of the
highest string; the lower sign refers
to the side of the lowest string.   71-C

Strike the side of the instrument,
    A. With fingertip.
    B. With knuckles.   61

Strike Body of Instrument (cont'd):

Play on the shoulder of the bass
A. With fingertips.
B. With palm of hand.
C. With the knuckles.
D. With the fingernails.
E. With the cupped hand. 45

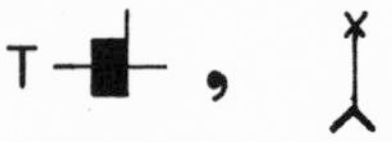

Strike the body of the instrument with the knuckles. 96-C; 119-C

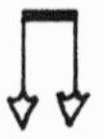

Tap on the body of the instrument with knuckles. 25-D

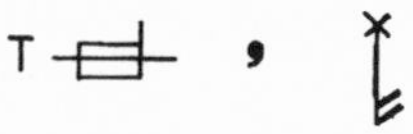

Slap the body of the instrument with the palm of the hand. 96-C; 105-A

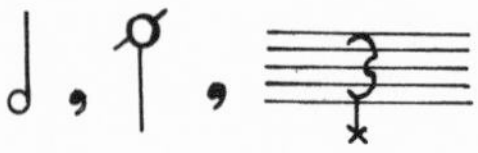

Strike the body of the instrument with the fingers or the palm of the hand. 19-A; 19-A; 119-C

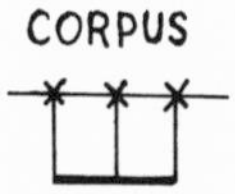

With the finger or open hand, strike the instrument at various places: sides, back, near the bridge, etc. 124

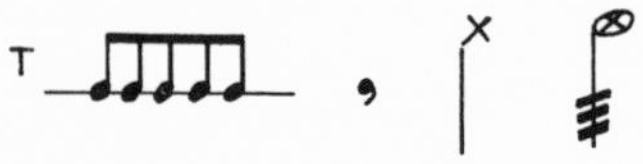

Drum on the body of the instrument with the fingertips. 96-C; 35; 35

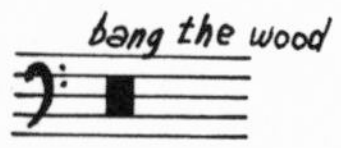

Tap or bang on the body of the instrument. 7-B

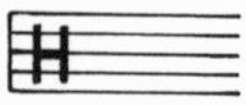

Strike the center back of the instrument with the hand; in the case of the double bass, strike with the flat of the hand near the shoulder of the instrument or beneath the bridge. 130-C

Strike the body of the instrument. 9

STRIKE BODY OF INSTRUMENT WITH BOW

⊓⊓⊓	Tap on the body of the instrument with the nut of the bow or tip of the finger.	89-E
₿	Use the heel of the bow on the belly of the instrument.	45
✖	Strike the body of the instrument with the bow.	19-A
✕	With the wood of the bow, strike the wood of the bridge.	19-C
┼┼┼┼┼┼┼┼┼┼┼┼	Place the hair of the bow on the back of the instrument, and roll the wood so that it hits the instrument.	61
⅄	Strike the peg of the instrument with the bow.	61
⅄	Strike the instrument with the bow from the side to the fingerboard.	61
⅄	With the bow, strike the scroll of the instrument.	61
⅄	With the nut of the bow, strike the chair or music stand.	119-C
⊓⊓⊓ , ⅄	Strike the music stand with the bow. 89-D; 9	

TREMOLO

	Tremolo.	42-B; 101-G
	A thick tremolo.	24-D
	A rapid, irregular tremolo on an open string.	89-F
	A rapid, irregular tremolo.	111-A
	Tremolo near the bridge for the duration of the dots.	45
	Oscillations made with a "shaky" bow.	9
	"Saw" with the bow.	89-D
	"Rub" with the bow.	89-D

VIBRATO

	Normal vibrato.	9, 6-B
	A great deal of vibrato.	9, 6-B
	A very narrow vibrato with two fingers.	9, 6-B

PERCUSSION AND HARP

CHAPTER III. PERCUSSION AND HARP

SYMBOLS FOR INSTRUMENTS

Abacus.		76
Mexican bean.		10-H
Large dog bark.		57-B
Bells:		
Church bell.		64
Bell for winding up (not alarm clock) (wind-up bell).		57-B
Glockenspiel, orchestra bells.		57-C
Cowbell (almglocken).		116-B; 57-C
Hand bell.		57-B
Jingle bell.		57-B
Sleighbells.		57-C; 116-B

Symbols for Instruments (cont'd):

Blocks:

	Temple blocks.	10-H; 57-C; 76
	Sand block.	10-H
	Wood block.	76; 72-A; 10-H
		72-B; 57-C
	Castanets, with and without handle.	57-B; 57-C
	Celesta.	10-H; 24-D
	Cencerros.	10-H
	Chains.	57-C

Chimes:

	Ceramic wind chimes.	101-E
	Glass wind chimes.	10-H; 76
	Grelots, hawk bells.	72-A

Symbols for Instruments (cont'd):

Chimes (cont'd):

   Tubular chimes.   10-H

   Wood wind chimes.   10-H; 72-A

   Claves.   57-C; 72-A

Cymbals:

                          Crotales.   72-A; 116-B; 57-C

     Diameter sign.   57-B

     Hand cymbals.   72-A; 57-B; 57-C

                          Hi-hat.   116-B; 10-H

   Suspended cymbals (sizzlers).
                                                                          57-C; 76; 10-H

                                              Suspended cymbals.
                                                62-C; 10-H; 116-B, 24-D; 57-B

     Dice case and dice.   57-B

Symbols for Instruments (cont'd):

Drums:

Bass drum, with and without foot
   pedal.   72-A; 57-B; 76; 10-H

Brake drum (automobile).   101-H

Bongos.   72-A; 116-B; 10-H

Bongo reversed with beans inside.   116-B

Chinese clatter drum.   57-B

Conga drum.   10-H

Wooden cylinder drum.   84-E

Log drum.   76; 10-H

African slit drum.   116-B

Snare drum.   57-B; 10-H; 24-D

                       72-A; 62-C, 116-B

Tablas.   10-H

Timpani.   10-H; 62-C; 64

Symbols for Instruments (cont'd):

Drums (cont'd):

African tom-tom.   72-A

Tom tom.   72-A, 62-C; 116-B, 62-C; 10-H

Tom tom (wooden membrane).   116-B

Drum with one wood and one skin
    membrane.   84-E

Drum with wood membranes.   84-E

Enclume (anvil).   72-B

Flexatone.   57-B

Gong:

Chinese gong.   10-H

Gong with dome center (Javanese).
                72-A, 116-B; 62-C

Guiro.   72-A; 57-C; 116-B

          10-H; 76

A. Hand clap.   10-H
B. With the hand.   116-B
C. Clapping of hands.   73

Harp.   24-D

Symbols for Instruments (cont'd):

 Harpsichord.   24-D

 Lujon.   10-H

 Maracas.   57-C; 72-B; 10-H, 76

 Marimba.   10-H; 72-B

 Marimbaphone.   116-B; 57-B; 10-H

 Piano.   3

 Ratchet.   57-B; 57-C

 Twisted metal rod or auto spring.   101-D

 Musical saw.   101-H

 Metal sheet (thunder sheet).   57-C

 Sistrum.   57-B

   Tambourine.   57-C; 57-C; 10-H; 72-B

Symbols for Instruments (cont'd):

Tam-tam.   72-A; 116-B; 64

                                                24-D; 76; 10-H

Triangle.   10-H; 62-C, 72-B; 57-C

Vibraphone.   76; 10-H

Washboard.   76

Whip.   57-C

Police whistle.   57-B

Xylophone.   10-H

A Percussion Set-Up.   101-E, D

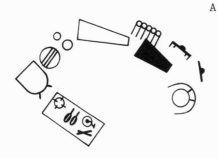

MALLETS

When the symbol for the mallet is up-
right, play with the normal end of
the mallet.   37-B, 64, 101-E, D

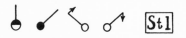

When the symbol for the mallet is reversed, play with the handle.
                     37-B, 64, 101-E, D; 22-A; 57-D

The arrow and the X indicate the part
of the mallet handle which is to strike
the instrument.   89-E; 100-D

                                              73; 62-C

Free choice of stick or mallet.   57-D

Play with two sticks in one hand.   57-D

A large symbol indicates a larger
mallet.   101-E, D

A small symbol indicates a normal or
small mallet.   101-E, D

Mallets (cont'd):

  Symbols

                        Arco, double bass bow.   98; 101-D

   Jazz brush. 64; 57-C; 89-B; 19-B; 19-B; 57-D

                        Metal or hoop end of wire brush.   92

   Wire brush.   64; 24-B; 76

                        Hard hair brush.   111-A

                        Hard brush.   73

                        Soft bass drum beater.   22-A; 57-D

                          Gong or tam-tam beater.   72-B; 101-E

                        Tam-tam beater of hard rubber.   64

                        Iron beater.   116-B

                        Ordinary tam-tam beater.   106

Mallets: Symbols (cont'd):

Claves or a similar piece of wood.
72-A; 57-C; 57-D

Crotale.
72-A; 57-C

A. Wood cluster stick. 7-B
B. Metal cluster stick. 101-D

Iron comb. 76

Finger or fingers.   96-E, 122-C; 37-B; 57-C

With the finger nail.
57-D; 57-C; 96-E; 96-E; 96-E

Guiro stick. 22-A

Left hand. 57-C; 98; 10-C

Right hand. 57-C; 98; 10-C

Hand. 57-D; 122-C

Wood hammer. 72-B; 84-F

Hammer. 86-C

Mallets: Symbols (cont'd):

Metal hammer.	22-A; 84-F
Metal hammer or other object of heavy metal.	64
Glockenspiel hammer.	24-D
Small glockenspiel hammer.	57-C
Knife with a long blade, to scrape.	64
Knitting needle.	64; 73
Felt mallet.	84-E
Soft felt mallet: g is large, m is medium.	57-D
Soft fluffy mallet, bass drum type.	72-B
Soft rubber mallet.	57-B; 57-D; 3
Soft felt mallets.	14-B; 57-B

Mallets: Symbols (cont'd):

	Timpani stick.	92
	Soft vibraphone stick.	22-A
	Soft yarn mallets.	3
	Medium mallets.	72-B; 37-B; 101-E, D
	Mallet with leather head.	57-D
	Soft rubber mallet.	57-C
	Medium hard yarn mallet.	79
	Brass mallets.	101-E, D
	Small hard felt mallet.	57-D
	Hard felt mallets.	92; 14-B; 47-B
	Hard plastic mallet.	3

Mallets: Symbols (cont'd):

Porcelain mallets.   64; 44

    Hard rubber mallets.   57-D; 57-B; 3

    Hard yarn mallets.   92; 3

Xylophone mallet.   64

    Wood mallets.   86-C; 57-C; 96-E; 84-E

Metal mallet.   84-E

Maracas: first play with the handle
up; then play with the handle down.   72-B

Bundle of nails.   64

    A. Hard pick. B. Soft pick.   100-D

Plectrum.   73; 16-B

Mallets: Symbols (cont'd):

 Wood snare drum sticks.
                      72-B; 62-B; 57-B; 57-C; 76; 37-B

   3; 57-D

  Thin wooden sticks (rattan).   22-A

  Wood stick.   79

  Thimble.   76

 Triangle beaters.   84-E; 37-A; 100-D; 57-B

   72-B; 89-B; 14-B; 67-A; 18

                            57-D; 111-B; 64

  Thin metal beater.   22-A

  Tuning fork (quasi triangle beater).   119-C

Pedal for hi-hat, timpani, etc.   37-B

AREAS OF ATTACK

⊙ ⌣ M⌐ +   Strike in the middle (center).
                111-B; 18; 57-C, 113-B; 62-B

Strike in the center with the indicated
mallet or stick.   25-D; 80-A

Strike the instrument 2/3 of the distance between the center and the edge. 113-B

Strike midway between center and edge.   92

Strike the instrument 1/3 the distance
from the center to the edge.   113-B

Strike near the edge or rim.
                111-B; 113-B; 92; 18; 64

                            119-B

Strike the rim of the instrument.
                25-D, 80-A; 57-C

        91-A; 111-A; 89-E; 64; 22-A; 22-D

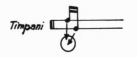

One mallet near the rim, and one mallet
in the center of the instrument.   59-B

Areas of Attack (cont'd):

Rimshot

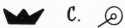

Rimshot.   57-B; 72-B; 89-D; 127; 24-B

22-D; 122-B; 113-C

Areas of Attack (cont'd):

Cymbals and Gongs

Strike the crown or dome.   127; 92; 25-D

MODES OF ATTACK

A. Glide to the left on playing surface.
B. Glide to the right.   57-C

The same as above, but begin without
audible attack.   57-C

Begin second note inaudibly.   57-C

Stroke radially, center to edge.   100-D

Modes of Attack (cont'd):

Circular Motion

↻	Rub or scrape in a semicircle, slower at the beginning (center).	37-B
⌒	Rub or scrape rapidly in a semi-circle.	37-B
⊙	Rub or scrape in a slow continuous circular motion.	37-B
	Strike around the edge of the instrument.	25-D
	Move in a very slow circular motion.	37-B
	Move in a circular motion from fast to slow.	37-B
	Move in a circular motion from slow to fast.	37-B
	Play in a circular motion, very slow.	72-B
Tam Tam / SUS CYM / Gong	Play in a circular motion on the in-dicated instruments for the indicated duration.	37-B

Modes of Attack: Circular Motion (cont'd):

Play in a circular motion on the sus-
pended cymbal with a jazz brush.   72-B

Play in a circular motion to the left
and retarding, then in a circular
motion to the right and accelerating.   57-C

Play in a circular motion on the gong
with hard mallets, let vibrate.   72-B

Agitate the cymbals in a sporadic
manner so as to simulate the line
pattern.   72-A

Beat on the indicated instrument in
an irregular circular manner with the
indicated beater.   72-B

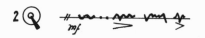

Rub the feet on the floor in a circular
manner.   97-A

Move the maracas in a circular manner;
line indicates duration.   10-H

Move the maracas in an expanding circular motion from slow to fast.   37-B

Modes of Attack (cont'd):

On the Hi-Hat

0	Strike, using the foot pedal; let vibrate.	127
∅	With hi-hat 1/2 open, strike with drum stick and let the two cymbals rattle together.	127
+	Slam closed with the foot pedal; do not let vibrate.	127
	Clash together; then immediately release and allow to vibrate.	96-E
	With the hi-hat already closed, strike with a stick.	96-E
	Strike with a stick while open.	96-E
	Hit with a stick while closed; then open instantly and allow to vibrate.	96-E

Modes of Attack (cont'd):

Rolls

	A roll (with one hand) consisting of as many single beats as the number indicates.	57-D
	An unmeasured roll.	41, 2-D, 22-A
	A measured roll (eight 32nds).	22-A

Modes of Attack: Rolls (cont'd):

	Roll.	122–D
		37–B
	Very slow roll or tremolo.	37–B
	A roll or tremolo that increases in speed.	57–D
	A roll or tremolo that decreases in speed.	57–D
	A roll.	76
	Perform a tremolo with the edge of the cymbal between the wires of a jazz brush.	14–B
	Roll or tremolo with the fingernails.	25–D
	Let stick bounce freely on the playing surface.	57–D

Modes of Attack (cont'd):

  Rubbing

	Rub in a circular manner.	76
	Rub the rim of the instrument with a stick.	119–C

Modes of Attack: Rubbing (cont'd):

Rub with the thumb.   122-D

Rub the thumb around or across the surface for the duration of the note.   127; 122-A

(hands) Rub hands together quickly.   96-A

Modes of Attack (cont'd):

  Scrape

Scrape the instrument for the duration
of the note value.   127

Scrape.   14-B

Scrape.   76

Strike or scrape.   64

Modes of Attack (cont'd):

  Shake

A. Shake rhythmically.   76
B. Shake or agitate.   122-A

Shake.   76

Modes of Attack (cont'd):

Strum

Strum the snares of the snare drum
in the directions indicated.   57-C

Modes of Attack (cont'd):

Striking

After having laid a drumstick on the
drumskin, strike the stick.   111-B; 89-D

Indirect hitting: hit a beater or
object previously placed on the
indicated surface.   57-C; 57-B

Strike on the housing, frame, or
casing of the instrument.   57-C

V

Strike at a right angle to the edge.   127

Play with one hand on each instrument.   68

Strike with two sticks simultaneously.   89-A

Double-stroke, the heel of the hand
followed by the fingers.   18

CLEFS AND STAVES

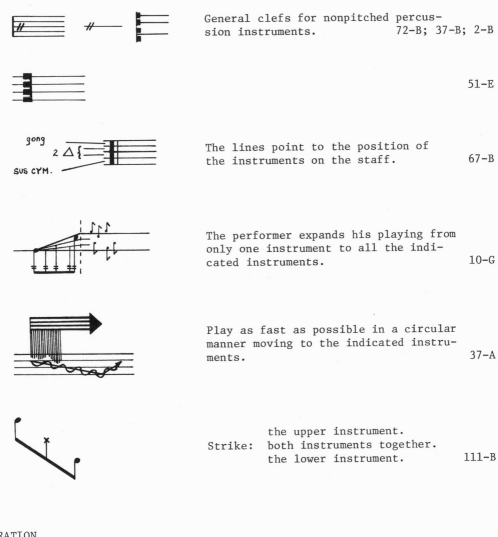

General clefs for nonpitched percussion instruments.   72-B; 37-B; 2-B

                                                                          51-E

The lines point to the position of the instruments on the staff.   67-B

The performer expands his playing from only one instrument to all the indicated instruments.   10-G

Play as fast as possible in a circular manner moving to the indicated instruments.   37-A

Strike: the upper instrument.
                  both instruments together.
                  the lower instrument.   111-B

DURATION

Staccato (always damp immediately).   57-C

Do not allow the mallet to spring back after the stroke; damp.   57-B

Depress pedal, and immediately release. 15-B

A note of short duration.   116-B

Duration (cont'd):

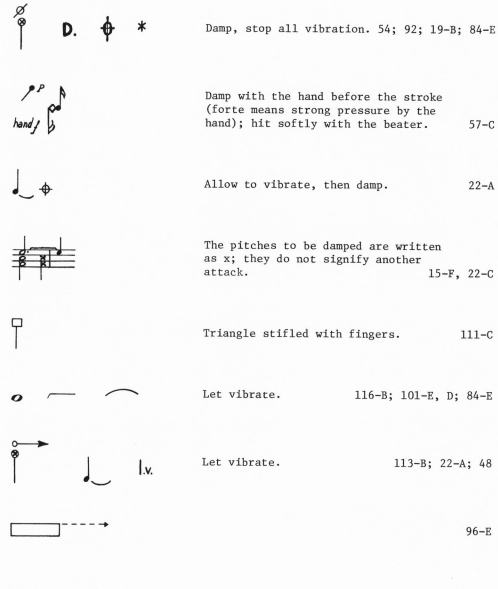

Damp, stop all vibration. 54; 92; 19-B; 84-E

Damp with the hand before the stroke (forte means strong pressure by the hand); hit softly with the beater.   57-C

Allow to vibrate, then damp.   22-A

The pitches to be damped are written as x; they do not signify another attack.   15-F, 22-C

Triangle stifled with fingers.   111-C

Let vibrate.   116-B; 101-E, D; 84-E

Let vibrate.   113-B; 22-A; 48

96-E

GLISSANDI

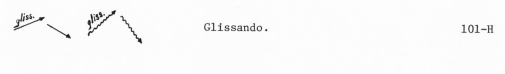

Glissando.   101-H

Glissando from center to edge.   25-D

Glissandi (cont'd):

 A glissando on wind chimes.

96-E; 10-H; 96-E; 10-H

 A tremolo cluster on glass chimes that is allowed to continue to vibrate. 31-A

 A stroke across the ridges of the guiro. 116-B

 Short glissando. 57-C

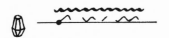 A continuous roll while making small glissandi (by changing pressure on head with heel of the hand). 10-H

 Pedal glissandi on the timpani. 101-D, E

 Glissandi on the musical saw. 71-E; 101-D, E

HARMONICS

 The diamond and the diamond notehead indicate harmonics. 89-E, 111-B; 62-B

 Harmonic: produced by striking near the edge of the instrument. 111-B, 89-E

KEYBOARDS, MALLET-TYPES, AND HARP

Chords

	The curved line indicates the order in which the notes should be played. 116-C
	The notes or clusters on the stems with the broken beam may be played in any order. 21-B
	A cluster whose limit is approximate in the direction of the arrow. 97-B
	Play the indicated number of "highest notes possible." 119-B
	Play the indicated number of "lowest notes possible." 14-A
	Play the indicated number of semitones in the area shown. 14-A
	Damp or release the cluster from left to right (lowest to highest pitches), so that the lowest notes are damped first. 15-F
	Play with the forearms. 71-B
	Play with the fist. 86-C; 57-D; 86-D
	Play or strike with the open palm. 86-C; 57-D

Keyboards, Mallet-Types, and Harp: Chords (cont'd):

                              Play or strike with the closed palm.   57-D

Play or strike with the fingertips.   57-D

Play or strike with the edge of the
hand.   57-D

Keyboards, Mallet-Types, and Harp: Chords (cont'd):

Duration

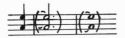   The notes in parentheses are to be
held and let vibrate.   15-F

   10-B

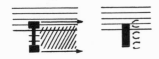   Clusters that are allowed to continue
vibrating.   100-E

Keyboards, Mallet-Types, and Harp: Chords (cont'd):

Played on Strings Only

                       Clusters of muted notes.   9

                Strike the strings with an open hand.
              10-E, 111-A, 47-B; 10-E, 96-C

                Strike the strings with the fist and
mallet.   86-C

DAMPING OR MUTING

Strings Only

♦	Damp the string with the hand before playing.	57-C
1 2 3	Damp within the first third (near damper) of the string, second third, third third.	57-D
⋈	Damp with the fingernail.	19-B
M	Mute with a finger on the string.	19-A
²◇	Damp with two or more fingers.	57-D
♩ 𝅘𝅥 𝆏	Stop the indicated string (x) from vibrating by damping with the hand.	73
0	Damp the strings with an object.	57-D
𝆏⁺	Mute the string with the left hand.	42-D
(( ))	Damp the string. ((= pizz.)	9, 6-B
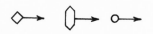	While damping, immediately glissando *along* the string or strings, not across the strings.	57-D

GLISSANDI

A double glissando into the bass clef area.

10-D

A cluster glissando, simultaneously in both directions.

57-D

A glissando cluster of semitones in an upward direction.

7-B

A series of arpeggiated chromatic clusters that keep rising.

66

A rapid arpeggio that moves toward the center from the outer two notes.

66

A glissando starting on the same note and moving in the directions indicated by the arrows.

70-A

A rapid glissando of the indicated notes.

72-B

Glissandi (cont'd):

On Strings Only

A powerful glissando, allowing the
strings to strike against each other.

96-E, 10-E, 122-D; 96-E

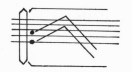

The elongated diamond refers to all of
the strings and is an indication to
damp while playing.   57-C

Play on the strings with a plectrum
in the indicated directions.   105-A

A four-finger cluster glissando played
in the direction and range indicated. 96-C

A slow glissando in the indicated
register.   65

A glissando played with the fingernail.   122-D

A fingernail glissando on the strings. 80-A

Glissandi: On Strings Only (cont'd):

A glissando on the strings with the
indicated stick.   104-A

A glissando with the palm of the hand
over the entire length of the strings
in the direction of the arrow.   10-E

Place the palm on the strings near the
damper; then play these notes in the
middle of the strings, making a quick
and powerful gliss in the direction
shown by the arrow.   10-E

Glissando on the strings in the indi-
cated range.   9; 10-H

A short glissando.   21-A

A smooth glissando across the strings.   11

A glissando across the strings, let-
ting the mallet bounce.   97-B

Play on the indicated strings, increas-
ing or decreasing the range as indi-
cated. (Always play rapidly.)   89-B

PIZZICATO

P pizz. ((G)	Pizzicato.	19-A; 57-D; 9
pizz. ↑↓↑↑	Pizzicato tremolo: strum the string in both directions.	67-A
	Pizzicato on the strings; pitches are indefinite.	89-A
	Indeterminate chords of two to four notes. The pitch is relative to the placement on the staff.	32-B
♀ ϕ ┴̅ φ	Pizzicato with a violent rebound of the string against the sounding board.	24-B; 57-E; 37-A; 70-A

Pizzicato (cont'd):

  Fingernail

⊲	Strike with the fingernail.	19-B
Ň o—	A right-hand pizzicato in which the string strikes the fingernail of the left hand.	24-B
○N ʌ↕↑ ⌒ r	Pluck with the fingernail.	3; 19-A; 96-C; 111-B
⊬	Place the fingernail against the vibrating string.	96-C
⊥	Flick the string with the fingernail.	96-C

Pizzicato (cont'd):

  Special Effects

                                             Pull with the soft part of the finger.   3

                                         Touch the string or instrument with a vibrating tuning fork (any pitch).   119-C

                                         Buzzing sound produced by string(s) vibrating against adjoining strings.   57-C

Pizzicato (cont'd):

  Strike Strings

                                         Strike the string.   9; 19-B

                                         Strike the indicated string with a stick.   80-A

                                         Strike any strings within the indicated range as fast as possible.
                                           A. With wooden sticks.
                                         B. With rubber sticks.
                                         C. With wire brushes.   80-A

                                         Strike the strings with the open hand.   73

RUB STRING

                                         Rub along the length of the string with the finger, plectrum, etc.   9

                                         Rub (glissando) along the string.   57-C

                                         Rub (glissando) with the key along one string. (Key = harp tuning key.)   19-B

                                         Rub vertically along one or more strings.   19-B

SCRAPE STRING

Scrape the string with a plectrum in
one direction.   73

Scrape along the string with the
fingernail, in the indicated direc-
tion.   7-A

Buzzing produced by a stroke with
another stick.   57-D

Scrape along the string with a plectrum
to produce a very rapid non-rhythmical
tremolo.   73

STRIKE CASE OR SOUNDING BOARD

Strike the sounding board with the
knuckles.   (C = corpus)   73

Strike the body of the instrument with
the knuckles.   10-E

Beat on the table immediately
    A. Before plucking.   57-C
    B. and D. While plucking.   57-C; 19-B
    C. After plucking.   57-C

Strike the sounding board with the
open hand.   19-B; 73

Strike the sounding board with the
finger.   19-B; 31-A

Strike the sounding board with the
indicated mallet.   19-B; 19-A

Strike the metal part of the instru-
ment with a metal rod.   19-B

Rub with the open hand on the sounding
board.   19-B

PIANO

Areas and Modes of Attack

RH LH	Right hand. Left hand.	100-D
RA LA	Right arm. Left arm.	100-D
	Staccato attack; then immediately de-press the key silently to retain a faint echo of the sound. 116-A; 57-D; 21-B	
	Depress the key completely, then gradually release. 116-A	
	Depress the key silently up to the jack; then force it sharply the rest of the way down. 21-B; 9	
	Depress the key silently. 116-A; 116-A; 57-C	
	Without depressing the keys, the tones are to be tapped with the fingernails or knuckles on the keyboard. 96-D	
	With a finger ring, strike the key without depressing it. 57-D	
	Produce a noise by striking the already depressed key. 57-D	
	Slam the lid, then lift it quickly. 19-A; 72-B	
	Strike the lid with the hand. 19-A	

Piano:　Areas and Modes of Attack (cont'd):

Beat on the body of the instrument
with the hands.　　　　　　　　　19-A

Strike the metal part of the instrument with a felt mallet.　　　　19-A

Indirect beating:　strike a stick that
is already on the strings or body of
the instrument.　　　　　　　　57-D

Piano (cont'd):

　Chords and Clusters

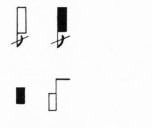

A cluster played with the arms within
the indicated limits.　　　　　23-B

A chromatic cluster.　　　　　21-A

Strike the indicated keys with the
open palm.　　　　　　　　　111-A

Clusters played on (A) white keys, or
(B) black keys with the fingers, palm,
or forearm.　　　　　　　　　65

Semitone clusters within the indicated
range: A. Staccato chord; B. Normal
duration.　　　　　　　　　7-B

Roll the cluster in the indicated direction.　　　　　　　　　　83

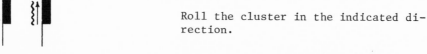

Play a cluster and release it gradually from the lower notes to the
highest.　　　　　　　　　57-C

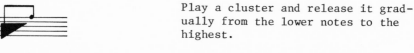

Clusters:　A. Free duration.
　　　　　　B. Measured duration.　67-A

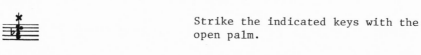

Piano: Chords and Clusters (cont'd):

Strike the keys with the forearm:
A. White keys. B. Black keys.   111-A

Roll the cluster with the forearm by
beginning with the elbow and quickly
bringing the entire forearm down.   24-C

Clusters that are semi-arpeggiated
either before the rhythm or after the
rhythm.   10-B

Play with the forearm.   57-D

Play with the forearm and hand.   57-D

Depress the keys successively, beginning with the wrist.   57-D

Depress the keys successively, beginning with the elbow.   57-D

Release the keys successively, beginning with the wrist.   57-D

Release the keys successively, beginning with the elbow.   57-D

Within the indicated limits, strike
the keys with the flat of the hand.   49-C

Clusters: inclination of the rectangle
refers to the position of the stick on
the strings.   57-D

With the palm of the hand, play clusters alternately on the white and
black keys.   7-B

Piano (cont'd):

    Damping or Muting

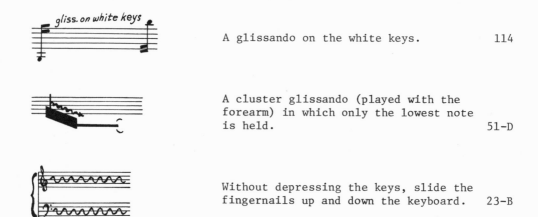

	Mute the indicated strings before depressing the keys. 4; 4; 24-C; 96-D
	Damp the string with the whole hand. 24-C
	Place a book on the indicated strings. 4
	Damp the string after depressing the key. 57-C
	Damp the string while depressing the key. 57-C
	Mute or stop the strings close to the damper while playing on the keyboard. 65
	For damping: p indicates little pressure; f indicates heavy pressure. 57-D

Piano (cont'd):

    Glissandi

	A glissando on the white keys. 114
	A cluster glissando (played with the forearm) in which only the lowest note is held. 51-D
	Without depressing the keys, slide the fingernails up and down the keyboard. 23-B

Piano (cont'd):

Harmonics

                     Harmonic: damp the indicated string
                           lightly.   57-C

◇   Harmonic: damp the string lightly,
                           close to the damper.   65

                     Fifth partial harmonic: Depress the
                           key while touching the string near
                           the damper.   31-A

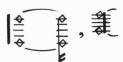   With the flat of the hand, silently
                           depress the indicated semitones. 49-C; 15-F

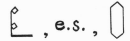   Depress the keys silently (e.s. =
                           enfoncer silencieusement).   73; 48; 57-D

                     Gradually release the silently de-
                           pressed cluster, beginning with the
                           lowest note.   57-C

Piano (cont'd):

Pedaling

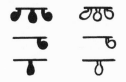   A. Depress the indicated pedal.
                           B. Release the indicated pedal.   9

                           Pedals: left, right, both.   111-A

                           Right pedal: depress . . . release.   111-B

Piano: Pedaling (cont'd):

Symbol	Description	Page
⌐ . _ . ⌐ , sus ped⎯⎯⎯⎯	Sustaining, prolongment pedal.	20, 10-B
𝒫𝒫𝑒𝒹.		57-C
⌐ _ _ _ ⌐ , ⌐ mid Ped. _ ⌐		109
L.P._._. , ⌐ _ _ _ ⌐	Una corda, left pedal.	116-A; 20
1C⎯⎯⎯⎯ , I.P.		10-B; 16-A
⌐·············⌐ , ꜀⎯⎯⎯		128-B; 76
fp	Attack the note; then depress the soft pedal as quickly as possible.	130
𝒫𝑒𝒹 ⎯⎯⎯⌐·⌐ / Ped⎯⎯⎯⌃	Depress pedal for the duration of the hold.	101-E, D
𝒫𝑒𝒹. ⎯⎯*	Hold pedal until the asterisk (*).	57-C
☰☰☰☰ (*)	Continue pedal for the indicated duration beyond the staff; then release gradually.	37-A
p⎯⎯⌐ , 𝒫𝑒𝒹↘ , 𝒫𝑒𝒹↘ *	Depress gradually.	3; 37-A; 2-B
Ped½ , Ped⅓	Depress pedal 1/2, 1/3 of the way down.	48
ⱷ	Depress the pedal just enough to maintain a soft tone after the key is released.	116-A
⎯⎯⎯⎯		93

Piano: Pedaling (cont'd):

Notation	Description	References
	Completely depress right pedal.	116-A; 20
Ped ⌐⌐⌐ ↗ Ped ⌐⌐⌐ ↗		93
Pedꟽꟽꟽ	Damp several times with the right pedal, but maintain some vibrations.	25-D
	Right pedal.	29; 76
		21-B
Ped----⋀--✶ ⋀	Right pedal: depress, release, depress.	51-E; 127, 37-B
		131
	Depress pedal; then release and quickly depress at each vertical stroke.	16-A
ped(9meas.) ——✶	Depress pedal for indicated number of measures.	34-E
Ped ——— ∿∿	Release the pedal in the approximate area indicated.	49-C
Ped —— ½→ Ped —— ½	Release gradually to 1/2 pedal.	96-D; 2-B
Ped ↗ Ped ↗✶	Release pedal gradually.	48; 15-F
		21-B, 22-A, 116-A; 9; 37-B
f ▷ *p* (dim with ped)	Diminuendo by gradually releasing pedal.	117

Piano: Pedaling (cont'd):

	Gradually release pedal, but keep key depressed. 116-A
	Staccato attack immediately followed by the pedal. 9
	Depress the pedal immediately after releasing the staccato note. 24-C
	Staccato attack, then immediately depress the right pedal so that the tone continues softly. 116-A
	16-A; 10-B
	After a sforzando, depress the pedal in such a way as to catch the resonances. 65
	Violently depress the sustaining pedal. 9; 7-B
	Release sustaining pedal quickly, causing it to bang. 9

Piano (cont'd):

Pizzicato

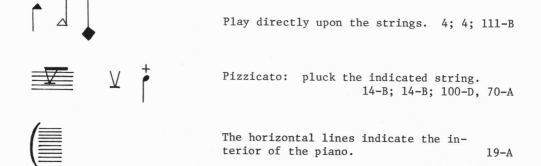

	Play directly upon the strings. 4; 4; 111-B
	Pizzicato: pluck the indicated string. 14-B; 14-B; 100-D, 70-A
	The horizontal lines indicate the interior of the piano. 19-A

Piano: Pizzicato (cont'd):

φ   φ

A violent pizzicato so that the string
strikes the sounding board.   96-C, 10-E; 70-A

Strike the string the indicated number
of times while moving in the direction
of the arrow.   57-D

Strike the string (with the fingernail)
away from the damper.   24-C

Drop a cylindrical box on the strings. 59-B

After striking a key, place a triangle
rod against the vibrating string.   119-B

Strike the already vibrating string
with the indicated mallet. Cease
striking at the arrow.   70-A

A pizzicato tremolo on the indicated
string with both hands.   70-A

Piano (cont'd):

  Registers

The piano is divided into four registers as defined by the framework of
the grand piano. Divergences from
the given ranges are, of course, to
be decided upon if the framework is
laid out differently.   73

The triple strings.

The bass strings, double and single.   59-A

The piano is divided into four ranges.
With the indicated mallet, play upon
the strings in the highest range.   89-E

HARP

Areas of Articulation

T , **T**——— , ⊔⊔⊔⊔   Play close to the sounding board.
                                        10-E, 111-D; 19-B; 47-B

ǐ , AT, ST , PT   Play close to the sounding board.
                                        12-E; 19-B; 86-D; 96-C

TD   Play close to the sounding board with
                       the fingers.   86-D

⌢   ⌢———⌐   Play close to the sounding board with
                       the fingernails.   50-B

TU , UT   Play close to the sounding board with
                       the fingernails.   86-D; 111-D

TD-C   Play close to the sounding board with
                       the fingers on the sounding board.   86-D

TU-C   Play close to the sounding board with
                       the fingernails on the sounding board. 86-D

UC   Play with the fingernails on the sound-
                       ing board.   86-D

TC   Beat the sounding board directly after
                       plucking the string.   86-D

φ   Play at the lower end of the strings,
                       letting the fingers slide immediately
                       and vigorously to the body of the
                       instrument.   96-C, 10-E

♦   Damp near the sounding board, and
                       play at the middle of the strings.   96-C

Harp: Areas of Articulation (cont'd):

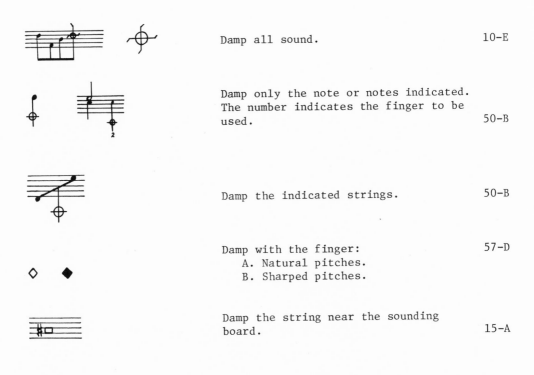

	Damp near the sounding board and play at the middle of the strings.	10-E
	Damp at the middle of the strings, and play near the sounding board.	10-E
M	Pluck the middle of the string with the fingertip.	111-D
UM	Pluck the middle of the string with the fleshy part of the finger.	111-D
PC ,	Play near the screws.	96-C, 19-B; 47-B

Harp (cont'd):

  Damping

	Damp all sound.	10-E
	Damp only the note or notes indicated. The number indicates the finger to be used.	50-B
	Damp the indicated strings.	50-B

	Damp with the finger:
	  A. Natural pitches.
	  B. Sharped pitches.
		57-D

	Damp the string near the sounding board.	15-A

Harp (cont'd):

  Glissandi

	Arpeggiate with four fingers.	73
	Arpeggiate with plectrum or finger.	73
	Strike (fast arpeggio) with plectrum or finger.	73
	A glissando that begins slowly, then accelerates. Let all tones vibrate.	51-D
	A glissando effect caused by a sweeping motion of the hand (away from the body) over the indicated strings; let fingernails touch the strings.	111-B
	Play along the string from the screw to the sounding board.	57-C
	Play along the string from the screw to the sounding board, and damp simultaneously.	57-C
	Glissando by turning the tuning key.	10-H

Harp (cont'd):

  Harmonics

                  Harmonics.   9; 19-A

Harp (cont'd):

Pedaling

Slashes above the line indicate flats,
on the line indicate naturals, below
the line indicate sharps.   57-C; 101-H

A. Pedals unchanged.
B. Pedals movable.   19-B

Stop the pedal in between the indicated
accidentals.   24-D

Place the relevant pedal between positions while the string is vibrating.   96-C

Glissando by changing the pedal.   19-B

                         57-C

                         72-B

Rapid and continuous change of the
designated pedals.   10-E

Change the pedal in a continuous
motion.   10-C

After plucking the string, depress the
pedal so that the vibrating string
strikes the tuning pegs.   119-C

MALLET-TYPE INSTRUMENTS

Damping

Do not allow the mallet to spring back
after the stroke; damp.   42-D

Damp.   10-E

Glissandi

Glissando with both hands in the
direction indicated.   10-H, 101-E

Glissando effect caused by a sweeping
motion of the hand in the direction of
the arrow and in the range notated.   111-B

Make the instrument vibrate gradually
in the indicated range by means of
quasi glissandi.   111-A

Glissando over the metal tubes.   111-A

Harmonics

A harmonic tone produced by damping
and hitting simultaneously.   57-C

Strike

Strike the indicated bars with the
smallest cymbal.   105-A

Strike the frame under the instrument. 105-A

Mallet-Type Instruments (cont'd)

Sustain

Sustain the pitch by humming or singing the pitch.   10-H, 101-D

VIBRAPHONE

Glissando

While holding the mallet at the node,
strike the bar. Then move the mallet
from the node to the center of the
bar.   101-D

Motor

m.a.

Motor on: numerals following m.a.
indicate rate of vibration. (1 lowest,
8 highest.)   44

m.s.

Motor off.   44

Vi
V

Vibrato.   24-B

molto ∿∿∿∿∿∿∿∿∿
vibr.

Much vibrato.   31-A

S.V.

Without vibrato. (Senza vibrato)   37-B

V. L.

Slow vibrato. (Vibrato lento)   37-B

Vibraphone: Motor (cont'd):

V. R.   Fast vibrato. (Vibrato rapido)   37-B

V. N.   Normal vibrato.   37-B

Motor on for the duration of the sign.   70-C

Pedal

Depress pedal for the duration of the
                                              sign.   101-E, D

Depress the pedal immediately after
immédiatement   the attack of the note.   15-B
Ped après l'attaque

WOODWINDS

CHAPTER IV. WOODWINDS

BREATH MARKS

L	Breath.	24-B
𝄔	Short breathing pause.	72-A, 65, etc.
𝄓	Very short breathing pause.	72-A, 56
⬦▭	Hold the tone until a breath is expired.	76
↓ ↓ ↓ +	Blow without producing a tone (air current noise).	44; 68; 76; 111-B
⬤ ×	Breathy tone (blowing-in effect).	52-C

AIR PRESSURE

⊕ ⊖	A. Blow harder. B. Blow easier.	120
N. Pr.	Normal air pressure.	6-A
M. Pr.	Much pressure.	6-A
A. Pr.	Augment air pressure.	6-A
D. Pr.	Diminish air pressure.	6-A
P. Pr.	Little pressure.	6-A

EMBOUCHURE

▼ ▽ 𝘯.   Embouchure on normal position of the
                  reed.   6-A; 6-B; 84-G

▽ ▽   Embouchure toward the tip of the reed.
                                                     6-A; 6-B

▽ ▽   Embouchure toward the base.   6-A; 6-B

▽   Move the reed in and out.   103

LIP PRESSURE

□ � ⌐⌐   Broken sounds (woodwind chords).
                  The signs under 'lip pressure' refer
                  to the production of woodwind chords.   6-A

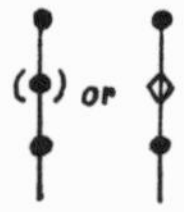

(♦) or ♦   Bracketed note or ♦ is subordinate
                  in the sound of the chord.   52-C

Reeds

○   Relaxed lip pressure.   6-A

⊙   Slightly relaxed lip pressure.   6-A

▭   Very relaxed lip pressure.   6-A

●   Increased lip pressure.   6-A

⊖   Slightly increased lip pressure.   6-A

▬   Much increased lip pressure.   6-A

Lip Pressure (cont'd):

Flute

O	Large aperture as for low register.	6-A
▭	Very wide, relaxed aperture.	6-A
⊖	Moderate aperture, middle register.	6-A
●	Small aperture, high register.	6-A
▬	Very small aperture, highest register.	6-A

GLISSANDI

	Bend the pitch up, then down.	42-A
	Bend the pitch down between 1/4 and 1/2 tone.	42-A
lento vibrato con ¼t	Slow vibrato with a 1/4-tone range down.	42-A
	Instrument plays regular note, and voice sings approximate note shown by the "x."	57-C
	Voice gliss while the instrument retains the same pitch.	57-C
	Play on the reed or mouthpiece only; then glissando by lip pressure.	7-A

KEY SOUNDS (CLICKS)

p
f

Dynamic below refers to the keys.
Dynamic above refers to the pitch.
(Key clicks-loud, pitch-soft)   44

Oblique stroke below a fingering
number means to half close the hole.   52-C

Strike the keys only, without use of
breath.   80-A; 24-B; 89-D

Strike the keys only, without use of
breath.   100-B, 76, 38; 100-B, 76, 38; 90-C

When tonguing, strike the key simultaneously.   111-B

Rattle the fingers rapidly on the
keys.   7-A

Move the keys (as many as possible)
without blowing into the instrument.   49-B

Trill by striking the keys only.   38, 7-B

MOUTHPIECE

Play on the mouthpiece in the indicated register.   119-B

Play on the mouthpiece only.   121; 89-D

Mouthpiece (cont'd):

Enclose the mouthpiece and the mouth
tightly with clenched fists, and then
gradually unclench them.   119-B

Strike the tube opening of the instrument with the open palm.   111-A

Remove the mouthpiece and blow into
the instrument.
    A. Flutter-tongue.   25-D
    B. Normal blowing.   121

TONGUING

Soft or throat attack.   126

A very soft windy attack.   126

Produce the sound by attacking the
sound in back of the throat.   25-A

Sharp attack, exaggerated "t" sound.   126

Attack as the spoken word "the."   126

Woodwind pizzicato: attack note, and
immediately stop air with tip of
tongue.   109; 24-B

Slap-tonguing: exaggerated attack.   121

Tonguing and making noises with the
keys.   25-A

Tonguing without producing a pitch.   25-D

Non-rhythmical tonguing, as fast as
possible.   25-A

Tonguing (cont'd):

   Flutter

Symbol	Description	Reference
	Flutter-tongue.	25-A; 111-A; 44; 76; 24-B
	Flutter-tonguing without producing a definite pitch.	25-D
	Flutter-tongue without sound.	25-A
	Flutter-tonguing on consonant "r."	111-B
	Cover the aperture with the lips and flutter-tongue.	119-B

FLUTE

   Blowing

Symbol	Description	Reference
	Blow to the opposite side of the mouthpiece; "not a full" sound, but definite pitch.	119-B
X	A kind of "fore-sound" produced by blowing a broad air stream at the mouthpiece from short distance.	59-B

   Glissando

Symbol	Description	Reference
	Use only the head joint; glissando by withdrawing the finger from the head joint of the flute.	105-A

Flute (cont'd):

Harmonics

  Harmonics. 24-B; 101-A; 84-G

  Harmonics on the same pitch, but different fingerings. 100-C

  Harmonics with different timbres (same pitch, different fingerings). 6-B

  Combine normal sound and harmonics. 89-A

  Trill from harmonic to natural, same pitch. 129

  Cover the aperture with the lips and blow so as to produce the desired harmonic ▣, stopping the sound quickly with the tongue ○. 119-B

OBOE

Brassy sound. 122-D

BRASS

CHAPTER V. BRASS

AIR STREAM EFFECTS

Play on the mouthpiece in the indi-
cated register.   119-B

Play only on the mouthpiece.
                              23-A; 121; 89-D; 104-A

Enclose the mouthpiece and the mouth
tightly with clenched fists, and then
gradually unclench them.   119-B

Slap the mouthpiece with the hand.   24-D

Tap (with the palm of the hand) on
the mouthpiece of the instrument in
any rhythm desired.   49-B

Blow directly into the instrument
without the mouthpiece.   121

Remove the mouthpiece and reverse it.
Holding it slightly away from the
instrument, blow to create a "swoosh"
sound.   25-A; 25-D

Breathy tone (blowing-in effect).
                                52-C; 52-C; 111-B

Strike the tube opening or the mouth-
piece with the open hand.   111-A

Blow into the instrument without pro-
ducing a tone.   68; 68; 49-B; 124

Air Stream Effects (cont'd)

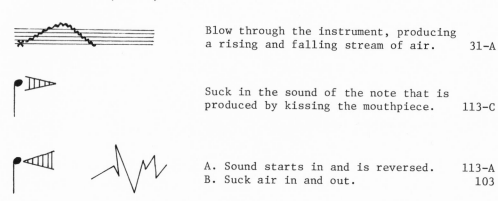

Blow through the instrument, producing a rising and falling stream of air.	31-A
Suck in the sound of the note that is produced by kissing the mouthpiece.	113-C
A. Sound starts in and is reversed.	113-A
B. Suck air in and out.	103

BREATH MARKS

Normal breath.	19-B, 57-C
Quick breath.	57-C, 19-B

GLISSANDI

A chromatic or articulated gliss, as opposed to the smooth gliss of a string instrument.	99
A fast half-step gliss.	122-B
A half-valve gliss.	113-C
Bend the pitch down to the indicated note and then up again.	42-A
A gliss to another note. Make the gliss as smooth as possible.	72-A

Glissandi (cont'd):

Oscillate, quasi tremolo.   91-A

Raise the pitch slightly for each
plus sign. The 'O' indicates regular
intonation.   105-C

Produce changes in timbre by a change
in fingering while maintaining a continuous air stream. The pitch remains
constant.   128-A

MUTES AND MUTING

Wawa   73

Straight   73

Plunger   73

Cup   73

Usually denotes tuba mute.   72-A

Use cupped hand to change the timbre.   103

A. Stopped   111-B
B. Stopped   116-D
C. Open   111-B, 116-D

A. Open gradually. B. Stop gradually.
                                        111-A, 73, 10-H

                                                82

                                                116-D

Mutes and Muting (cont'd):

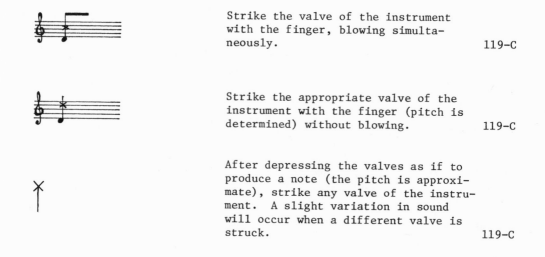

⊕ ⊕——┐	A. Not completely stopped (echo sounds). 8;3
	B. Half stopped. 79
CS	With mute (con sordino). 73
——→ hush	The conductor or one of the players places the mute in the instrument while the performer is still playing. 64
⟳/ ‖‖‖‖‖	Wawa effect. 73
◁	Flip with the fingers on the bell. (Tap on the bell.) 73
ϒ	Cuff with the hand on the embouchure. 73
S S or via sord.	Without mute (senza sordino). 73; 121

PERCUSSIVE EFFECTS

(staff notation)	Strike the valve of the instrument with the finger, blowing simultaneously. 119-C
(staff notation)	Strike the appropriate valve of the instrument with the finger (pitch is determined) without blowing. 119-C
✗	After depressing the valves as if to produce a note (the pitch is approximate), strike any valve of the instrument. A slight variation in sound will occur when a different valve is struck. 119-C

TONGUING

Flutter

	Flutter-tongue. 21-C; 66; 37-B, 97-A, 24-B
	Flutter-tongue. 25-D; 39; 76; 111-B
	Flutter-tonguing on the consonant "r." 111-B; 101-H
	Non-rhythmic, uneven flutter-tonguing, or uneven rapid tonguing. 89-B
	Flutter-tongue without sound. 25-A
	Flutter-tongue without producing pitch. 25-A
	Remove the mouthpiece and blow into the instrument; flutter-tongue without producing any pitch. 25-A
	Enclose the mouth-hole tightly with the lips and perform a frullato, flutter (the pitch is approximate). 119-C

Tonguing (cont'd):

Other Types

	Non-rhythmic, uneven tonguing, as fast as possible. 25-A

Tonguing: Other Types (cont'd):

ϕ
                                    Slap-tonguing: strike the mouthpiece
with the tongue.   21-B, 121

ΥΥΥΥ
                                    Tonguing without producing a pitch.   25-D

Υ
                                    Produce the sound by attacking the
sound in the back of the throat.   25-A

(hd) or (td)
                                    Ways of articulating the beginnings
and endings of notes (h or t at be-
ginning and d at end).   52-C

m
                                    Tone with humming noise (humming tone,
guttural sound, static of any chosen
pitch).   52-C

didl
                                    Double-tonguing (as a timbre-forming
element).   52-C

VIBRATO

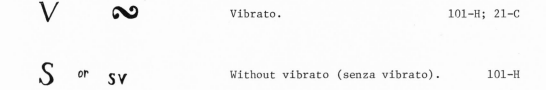

V   ∾
                                    Vibrato.   101-H; 21-C

S   or   sv
                                    Without vibrato (senza vibrato).   101-H

VOICE

CHAPTER VI. VOICE

GLISSANDI AND VIBRATO

	Glissando.	51-C
	A glissando into the lower register. The dynamic level is indicated by the heavy line below the staff.	101-B
	Glissando by changing lip position.	59-A
	Intonation contour. Pitch is shown by the jagged line; the slashes indicate a fluttering sound.	10-A
	A slow, wide vibrato.	72-A

MOUTH EFFECTS

	Mouth closed (bocca chiusa).	89-C; 84-D; 24-D; 10-A
b.ch. , b.c.,	Mouth open halfway.	24-D; 15-A; 72-A
+ (mouth open halfway)		
a.a.	Mouth slightly open (appena aperta).	84-D
	Mouth open.	24-D
	Mouth open, then closed.	72-A
	Sotto voce to open mouth.	45

Mouth Effects (cont'd):

Bi ———▷ + b.f.   Begin with the mouth open, then close
                        it (bouche fermée).   15-A

— — — — — (*closing the mouth*) +   Gradually close the mouth.   86-B

(b.c.)   (a.a.)   The broken line is used to connect the
                        articulation from closed mouth (b.c.)
                        to slightly opened mouth (a.a.).   84-C

HAND OVER MOUTH

CJ   Close mouth almost completely with hand.   58

C/   Half-close mouth with hand.   58

C—   Remove hand from mouth.   58

C⟩   Cup hand in front of mouth.   58

(hm)   Hand (or hands) over mouth.   10-A

(hm)ᵚ   Moving cupped hand over mouth to af-
                        fect sound (like a mute).   10-A

(hd)   Hands down. Remove hands from mouth.   10-A

+++   Tapping very rapidly with one hand (or
 ≣   fingers) against the mouth (action
                        concealed by other hand).   10-A

⟩— – →   A gradual transition (a ⟩— – → il).   58

                        Pat the mouth with the hand in a con-
                        tinuous motion, changing the character
                        of the sound.   96-A

SINGING VOICE

Specific Pitch

A   Sing.   98

On the five-line staff, the intervals
are to be sung precisely, but the
phrases may be transposed.   10-A

Singing voice, produced in the normal
manner.   68; 68

Singing Voice (cont'd):

Approximate Pitch

A. Sing.   57-C, 19-A
B. Sing, as short as possible.   10-A

Sing, fixed pitch.   51-C; 51-C

Sing, pitch approximate.   51-C

51-C; 51-C

10-H; 60; 58; 58

Sing; relative register is indicated
by the three-line staff.   10-A

SINGING VOICE TO SPEAKING VOICE

Attack the sound on the exact pitch;
then change the voice to speaking. Do
not change the pitch.   15-D

SPEECH-SONG (SPRECHSTIMME)

	Sung on the breath.	10-H
	Half-voice, quasi recitative.	89-A
	Voiced, but breathy. No definite pitch.	44
	Speech-song with fixed pitches.	68; 68
	Speech-song.	57-C, 107-A
	Almost singing, but allow the voice to remain indefinite, somewhat like the harmonics of a string instrument.	15-D
	Sotto voce.	33-B
	Speech-song, sprechstimme.	51-C
	Speech-song, tied notes.	51-C
	Speech-song, relative pitch.	51-C
	A. Voice raised. B. Voice lowered. Pitch varies with the size of the letter(s).	51-C

	Melodization of speech, bordering on chanting:
	    A. Voice lowered.
	    B. Voice raised.
		51-C

	Speech-song with changing, but not definitely fixed, pitches. (The horizontal line corresponds to the middle register of the singer.)	68; 68

SPOKEN TEXT

Specific Pitch

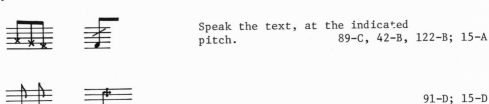

Speak the text, at the indicated
pitch.   89-C, 42-B, 122-B; 15-A

91-D; 15-D

Spoken Text (cont'd):

Approximate Pitch

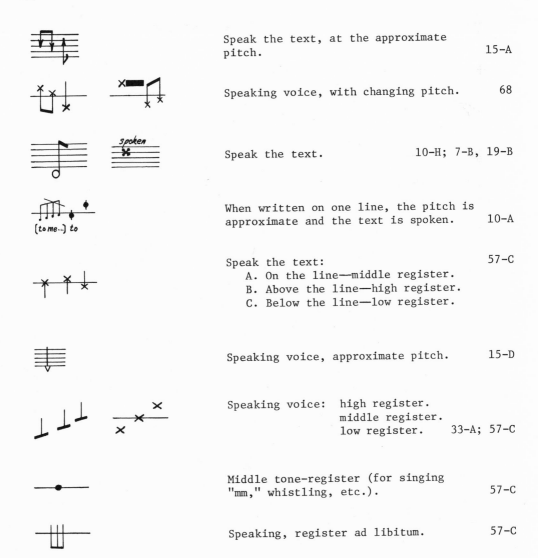

Speak the text, at the approximate
pitch.   15-A

Speaking voice, with changing pitch.   68

Speak the text.   10-H; 7-B, 19-B

When written on one line, the pitch is
approximate and the text is spoken.   10-A

Speak the text: 57-C
A. On the line—middle register.
B. Above the line—high register.
C. Below the line—low register.

Speaking voice, approximate pitch.   15-D

Speaking voice: high register.
                 middle register.
                 low register.   33-A; 57-C

Middle tone-register (for singing
"mm," whistling, etc.).   57-C

Speaking, register ad libitum.   57-C

Spoken Text: Approximate Pitch (cont'd):

Plain stems denote the rhythm of the
spoken text.   33-B, 49-A

Speak the letters or text.   89-E

TIMBRE EFFECTS

Audible inhaling, gasping.   10-A; 51-C

Breathe audibly.   19-A

Exhale audibly.   19-A; 51-C

Very intensive but unvoiced breathing:
   A. Inhaling.
   B. Exhaling.   68

A speaking voice simultaneously with
inhaling.   68

Sing in a creaky voice.   101-F

Cough.   10-A

Falsetto.   57-C, 94-B; 89-C, 60

Hi   98

HA   98

Timbre Effects (cont'd):

⚲ (head voice symbol)	Head voice with exaggerated lip movements.	57-C
AA	A very light, clear sound.	98
R - - - - - - -	A kind of flutter-tongue.	59-A
——— - - - - -	A gradual transition to flutter-tongue.	59-B
()()()() r	Rapid alternation of overly rounded to overly spread lips on the indicated sound.	101-A
r	Heavily rolled "r."	96-B
r ▬▬▬▬	Flutter-tongue, a kind of song frullato. Pitch is shown by the shape of the horizontal line.	51-C
r〜〜MMM	Fluttered "r" changing into a sucking sound.	45
ʔ , a'	A. Glottal stop. B. A glottally stopped "a."	10-A 101-F
Ⓐ	Sound coming from the throat.	98
ϙ	Cry, shout.	19-A
L	Laughter.	10-A
╪╪	Laughing: high, low.	51-C

Timbre Effects (cont'd):

s ▱▱▱▱▱▱	A hissing sound on "s." Pitch is shown by the horizontal line.	51-C
sh ▱▱▱▱▱	A hissing sound on "sh." Pitch is shown by the horizontal line.	51-C
Ⓕ〜 Ⓢ〜	A hissing sound on the indicated consonant.	97-A
(hum)	Square noteheads indicate that the pitch is to be hummed.	7-B
M [ʔ]	Mouth click.	45; 10-A
～	Nasalised.	68, 101-F
⌀	Lip pop or tongue cluck.	96-B
▼ ▼ᶠ ,	A shout at the approximate pitch indicated.	58
↑ ↑ ↑ ↑	A gradual transition from speaking to shouting.	58
⊥	Throaty, unarticulated voice without resonance.	51-C
⸮	Tongue cluck.	57-C
↓	Click the tongue.	51-C
≡	Tremolo.	10-A

Timbre Effects (cont'd):

(symbol)	Dental tremolo or jaw-quivering.	10-A
S — — — —	Tremolo produced by trembling the lower jaw.	59-A
(diagram)	A tremolo that alternates between the indicated sounds. The increasing size of the noteheads signals a crescendo, and the closer spacing signals an accelerando.	101-F
~✗	Trill the tongue against the upper lip.	10-A
(symbol)	Weeping.	51-C
+, o, o—	Breathy tone, almost whispered.	10-A
$, (symbols)	Whisper.	60; 58
φ	Whispered sound, as short as possible.	10-A
O , X	Unvoiced sounds, whispered.	10-A; 96-B
(symbols) or (symbols)		68; 68
(symbols)	Half-note value is indicated by two tied quarter-note stems.	68
(whisper) (staff)	Whisper the indicated pitch.	7-B

Timbre Effects (cont'd):

WHAT   Hollow letters or words indicate
                        whispering.   100-D

○   When above or below an otherwise voiced
V ———→ V   sound, the symbol indicates that the
  ○   sound is unvoiced:
V ———→ V   A. Unvoiced.
       ○   B. Unvoiced to voiced.
                            C. Voiced to unvoiced.   68

                        Unvoiced, no pitch.   44

                        Murmur.   58

         or   Murmuring at various pitches.   68

    ,   ◇   Murmur, whisper.   60; 19-A

                                                            68

P   The upper dynamic refers to the inten-
[*ff*]   sity of the voice. The bracketed dy-
                        namic refers to the intensity of the
                        simultaneous breath.   68

F, 𝄐F   Whistle.   19-A

                                                            58

TEXTUAL EFFECTS

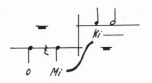

The curved line indicates the movement of syllables or words of the text from one part to another.

34-B

The dotted line serves the same function as the curved line above.

84-D

The arrow serves the same function as the lines in the above two examples.

123

$\left(\begin{array}{c} a \\ /tru/ \\ to \\ me \end{array} \right)$

Sounds and words lined up in parentheses must be repeated quickly in a random and slightly discontinuous manner.

10-A

(to me...) , (be/lo/...)

Groups of sounds and words in parentheses must be repeated quickly in a regular way for the indicated duration.

10-A

[a] , [ka], [u]

(See the section on phonetics.) Sounds or groups of sounds that are phonetically notated.

10-A

/gi/, /wʊ/

Sounds or groups of sounds as pronounced in context, e.g., /gi/ as in <u>gi</u>ve.

10-A

Textual Effects (cont'd):

A text chosen by the performer is to be sung freely for the duration of the dotted line.

57–C

A. Voiceless consonant.
B. Voiced consonant.

98

Hold the underlined consonant.

89–A

Whisper the syllable "re" for the duration of the hold.

86–A

Hold the "a" sound for the duration of the arrow.

34–B

Portions of the text preceded by a line should be articulated as if in a slur.

112

Subscript text in parentheses is a guide to pronunciation and consists of phonetic symbols or phonetic spellings of text.

112

Superscript in parentheses indicates final or initial consonants which are not to be pronounced (in that part), but which appear as a guide to pronunciation.

112

The raised vowel next to a consonant indicates that the vowel is heard allusively after full articulation of the consonant.

68

Textual Effects (cont'd):

A₀ | The "A" blends slowly into the "o." | 98

⟶ or ⟶ ⟶ | A continual, even transition without an interruption of the tone. | 68

m⟶o | | 57-C

R ⁽ᵒ→ᵋ⁾ | The cursively indicated phonetic signs in parentheses should be articulated by lip movements at the same time as the main sound. | 57-C

u - -no   m'écouter | The squared syllables are to be held and blended into either spoken or sung text depending on how the previous text was rendered. | 86-A

| The dotted line indicates that the pitch remains constant while the vocal color changes. | 10-A

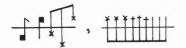

| The pitch is indicated by the relative height of the letters on the page, while the dynamics are indicated by the thickness of the letters. (Thick = forte, thin = piano) | 100-D

| A succession of different symbols within the same musical phrase indicates a gradual transition from one articulation to another. | 68

PHONETIC SOUNDS

The sounds of the following letters are represented by their usage in the
accompanying words.   10-A, 101-A, F, B, 10-H

e	'a' in hay, say.		**r**	'r' in rich.
a	'a' in lack, black.		**rr**	Spanish rolled 'r.'
ɑ	'a' in car, bar.		**ʃ**	'sh' in sheep, ship.
ɔ	The sound of 'awe.'		**s**	's' in see.
b	'b' in boy.		**ʒ**	's' in leisure.
d	'd' in dog.		**t**	't' in toy, top.
i	'ee' in see.		**ð**	'th' in them.
ɛ	'e' in den, pen.		**θ**	'th' in thing.
g	'g' in go.		**u**	'u' in sue, blue.
ɦ	'h' in manhood, behead.		**ʊ**	'u' in German *unter*.
ɩ	'i' in hit, lit.		**ø**	'eu' in French *meuble*
k	'k' in keep.		**Y**	'u' in German *mutter*.
ł	'l' in fable, label.		**ʌ**	'u' in cup.
n	'n' in not.		**w**	'w' in will.
ɲ	'gn' in Italian *Bologna*; 'n' in Spanish *señor*.		**φ**	'w' in German *schwester*.
ɱ	'n' in Italian *invidia*.		**x**	'x' in Spanish *Mexico, Oaxaca*.
ŋ	'ng' in cling, ring.		**j**	'y' in yesterday.
o	'o' in glow, boat.		**ʎ**	'gl' in Italian *intaglio*.
			z	'z' in zero.

LIST OF COMPOSERS CITED

(Publication date follows title. Composition date is in parentheses.)

1. Aitken, Hugh
   Piano Fantasy, 1969

2. Amy, Gilbert
   A. *Triade*, 1967
   B. *Cahiers d'Épigrammes*, 1966
   C. *Diaphonies*, 1965
   D. *Mouvements*, 1959

3. Andrus, Donald
   Imbrications, 1967

4. Antoniou, Theodor
   Lyrics, for piano and violin, 1968

5. Bark, Jan
   Pyknos, 1968

6. Bartolozzi, Bruno
   A. *New Sounds for Woodwind*, 1967
   B. *Quartetto per archi*, 1960

7. Bedford, David
   A. *That White and Radiant Legend*, 1967
   B. *Music for Albion Moonlight*, 1966

8. Benhamou, Maurice
   Mizmor 114, 1967

9. Benvenuti, Arrigo
   Folia (1963)

10. Berio, Luciano
    A. *Sequenza III*, 1968
    B. *Sequenza IV*, 1967
    C. *Rounds for Harpsichord*, 1966
    D. *Passagio*, 1966
    E. *Sequenza II*, 1965
    F. *Sincronie*, 1964
    G. *Tempi Concertati*, 1962
    H. *Circles*, 1961
    I. *Nones*, 1955

11. Bertoncini, Mario
    Cifre

12. Birtwistle, Harrison
    A. *Punch and Judy*, 1968
    B. *Tragoedia*, 1967
    C. *Entr'acts and Sappho Fragments*, 1965
    D. *Précis*, 1965
    E. *The World Is Discovered*, 1963

13. Boehmer, Konrad
    Potential for Klavier (1961), 1968

14. Boguslawski, Edward
    A. *Apokalypsis*, 1967
    B. *Kinoth Na Orkiestre*, 1963

15. Boulez, Pierre
    A. *Le Soleil des Eaux*, 1968
    B. *Pli selon Pli*, 1967
    C. *Éclat*, 1965
    D. *Le Visage Nuptial*, 1964
    E. *Improvisation sur Mallarmé I*, 1958
    F. *Improvisation sur Mallarmé II*, 1958

16. Braun, P. Michael
    A. *Thesis*, 1968
    B. *Monophonie*, 1967

17. Brown, Earle
    Available Forms I, 1962

18. Burge, David
    Sources III, 1968

19. Bussotti, Sylvano
    A. *Il Nudo*, 1964
    B. *Fragmentations pour un Joueur des Harpes*, 1963
    C. *Phrase à Trois*, 1962

20. Cage, John
    Music of Changes, 1961

21. Cardew, Cornelius
    A. *Four Works*, 1967
    B. *Books of Study for Pianists*, 1966
    C. *Autumn 60*, 1960

22. Carter, Elliot
    A. *Double Concerto for Harpsichord and Piano*, 1961
    B. *Quartet, Strings, no. 2* (1959), 1961
    C. *Recitative and Improvisation for 4 Tympani*, 1960
    D. *Variations for Orchestra*, 1957

23. Castiglioni, Niccolò
    A. *Alef: Komposition für Oboe*, 1967
    B. *Consonante* (1962), 1963
    C. *Aprèsludo*, 1960
    D. *Cangianti per Pianoforte*, 1959

24. Cerha, Friedrich
    A. *Mouvements I-III*, 1968
    B. *Enjambements* (1959), 1963
    C. *Deux Éclats en Reflexion*, 1964
    D. *Relazioni Fragili* (1957), 1960

25. Cervetti, Sergio
    A. *Pulsar*, 1969
    B. *Zinctum, für Streichquartet*, 1969
    C. *Fünf Episodem*, 1968
    D. *Six Sequences for Dance*, 1967

26. Chou, Wen-Chung
    And the Fallen Petals, 1955

27. Clementi, Aldo
    Triplum, 1961

28. Corghi, Azio
    Stereofonie X4, 1967

29. Cozzella, Damiano
    Discontinuo, 1966

30. Croley, Randell
    Mies Structure #3, 1970

31. Crumb, George
    A. *Echoes of Time and the River*
    B. *Sonata, violoncello*, 1958

32. Curran, Alvin S.
    A. *First Piano Piece*, 1967
    B. *Thursday Afternoon*, 1967

33. Dallapiccola, Luigi
    A. *Canti di Liberazione per coro misto e grande orchestra*, 1955
    B. *Volo di Notte*, 1952

34. Davies, Peter Maxwell
    A. *Sinfonia*, 1968
    B. *Five Motets*, 1966
    C. *O Magnum Mysterium*, 1962
    D. *String Quartet*, 1962
    E. *5 Pieces for Piano, op. 2*, 1958

35. Druckman, Jacob
    String Quartet #2, 1966

36. Eder, Helmut
    Konzert für Fagott und Kammerorchester, 1968

37. Eloy, Jean Claude
    A. *Etudes III*, 1965
    B. *Equivalences*, 1965

38. Evangelisti, Franco
          Proporzioni (1958), 1961

39. Feldman, Morton
          In Search of an Orchestration, 1969

40. Fellegrara, Vittorio
          Mutazioni, 1964

41. Finney, Ross Lee
          Concerto for Percussion and Orchestra, 1966

42. Foss, Lukas
          A. *24 Winds*
          B. *Fragments of Archilochos*, 1966
          C. *Elytres*, 1965
          D. *Echoi*, 1964

43. Fukushima, Kazuo
          Three Pieces from "Chu-U," 1964

44. Gaber, Harley
          Voce II, 1967

45. Gaburo, Kenneth
          Inside

46. Gandini, Gerardo
          Musica Nocturna, 1966

47. Górecki, Henryk M.
          A. *Muzyczka 2*, 1968
          B. *Monologhi*, 1962
          C. *I Symfonia "1959,"* 1961

48. Guyonnet, Jacques
          Polyphonie I, 1968

49. Halffter Jiménez, Cristóbal
          A. *In Exspectatione Resurrectionis Domini*, 1967
          B. *Lineas y Puntos*, 1967
          C. *Sinfonia para tres grupos instrumentales*, 1963
          D. *5 Microformas, para orchestra*, 1962

50. Harrison, Lou
          A. *Suite for Symphonic Strings*, 1961
          B. *Suite for Violoncello and Harp*, 1954

51. Haubenstock-Ramati, Roman
          A. *Klavierstücke I*, 1966
          B. *Jeux 6* (1960), 1965
          C. *Credentials*, 1963
          D. *Petite Musique de Nuit*, 1963
          E. *Sequences*, 1961
          F. *Staendchen, sur le nom de Heinrich Strobel*, 1958

52. Heider, Werner
    A. *Inneres, für orgel*, 1969
    B. *Da Sein*, 1966
    C. *Katalog für einen Vibraphonspieler*, 1966

53. Holliger, Heinz
        Mobile, 1964

54. Horváth, Jósef Mária
        Redundanz 2, 1967

55. Johnston, Ben
        Seven

56. Jolas, Betsy
        D'un Opera de Voyage, 1968

57. Kagel, Mauricio
    A. *Pas de Cinq*, 1967
    B. *Match*, 1967
    C. *Anagrams* (1957/58), 1965
    D. *Transición II* (1958/59), 1963
    E. *Sexteto* (1953), 1962

58. Karkoschka, Erhard
        Homo Sapiens (1968), 1969

59. Kilar, Wojciech
    A. *Diphthongos*, 1965
    B. *Générique*, 1964

60. Koszewski, Andrzej
        La Espero, 1965

61. Kotik, Petr
        Musik für Drei, 1965

62. Kotonski, Wlodzimierz
    A. *Kwintet*, 1966
    B. *Musica per Fisti e Timpani*, 1964
    C. *Canto*, 1962

63. Kruyf, Ton de
        Einst dem Grau der Nacht Enttaucht, 1964

64. Kupkovic, Ladislav
        Mäso Križa, 1965

65. Lanza, Alcides
        Plectros II, 1966

66. Levy, Marvin D.
        Kyros, 1966

67. Lidholm, Ingvar
    A. *Poesis, per orchestra*, 1966
    B. *Mutanza, per orchestra*, 1961

68. Ligeti, György
        Aventures, 1964

69. Logothetis, Anestis
        Dynapolis, 1967

70. Maderna, Bruno
    A. *Honeyrêves per flauto e pianoforte*, 1963
    B. *Concerto for Oboe*, 1962
    C. *Serenade #2*, 1957

71. Mayuzumi, Toshirō
    A. *Prelude, string quartet*, 1964
    B. *Bacchanale*, 1960
    C. *Metamusica*, 1961
    D. *Nirvaña-Symphonie*, 1958
    E. *Pieces for Prepared Piano and Strings*, 1958

72. Mefano, Paul
    A. *Lignes*, 1968
    B. *Paraboles d'Après Yves Bonnefoy*, 1968

73. Mellnäs, Arne
        Tombola, 1968

74. Mendes, Gilberto
        Nasce Morre, 1966

75. Messiaen, Olivier
        Couleurs de la Cité Céleste, 1966

76. Miroglio, Francis
        Phases, 1968

77. Moevs, Robert
        String Quartet, 1967

78. Moran, Robert
        Four Visions, 1964

79. Moss, Lawrence
        Remembrances, 1969

80. Moszumanska-Nazar, Krystyna
    A. *Variazioni Concertanti*, 1967
    B. *Muzyka Na Smyczki*, 1964

81. Mumma, Gordon
        Small Size Mograph, 1964

82. Nikiprowetzky, Tolia
        Adagio, 1964

83. Nobre, Marlos
        Ukrinmakrinkrin, 1968

84. Nono, Luigi
        A. *Per Bastiana Tai-Yang Cheng*, 1967
        B. *Canti di Vita e d'Amore*, 1963
        C. *Ha Venido*, 1960
        D. *Sarà Dolce Tacere*, 1960
        E. *Composizione per Orchestra*, nr.2, 1959
        F. *Cori di Didone*, 1958
        G. *Variations*, 1957

85. Otte, Hans
        Tropismen, *für Klavier*, 1963

86. Paccagnini, Angelo
        A. *Actuelles*, 1968
        B. *Vento nel Vento*, 1967
        C. *Gruppi Concertanti*, 1963
        D. *Musica da Camera*, 1961

87. Palester, Roman
        Metamorphoses, 1968

88. Pärt, Arvo
        Perpetuum Mobile, 1968

89. Penderecki, Krzysztof
        A. *Capriccio, per oboe e 11 archi*, 1968
        B. *Capriccio, per violin ed orchestra*, 1968
        C. *Passion According to St. Luke*, 1967
        D. *Fluorescences*, 1962
        E. *Dimensionen der Zeit und der Stille*, 1961
        F. *Emanationen*, 1960
        G. *Strofy*, 1960

90. Pennisi, Francesco
        A. *Fossile*, 1968
        B. *Palermo, Aprile*, 1968
        C. *Quintetto*, 1965

91. Petrassi, Goffredo
        A. *Musica di Ottoni*, 1964
        B. *Propos d'Alain*, 1962
        C. *Quartet, strings*, 1958
        D. *Quattro Inni Sacri*, 1946

92. Phillips, Peter
        Music for Percussion, 1968

93. Pousseur, Henri
        Madrigal 3, 1966

94. Powell, Mel
        A. *Filigre Setting*, 1965
        B. *Haiku Settings*, 1961

95. Powell, Morgan
              Sirhmrej, 1967

96. Rands, Bernard
              A. *Sound Patterns I*, 1968
              B. *Sound Patterns 2*, 1968
              C. *Formats I*, 1966
              D. *Espressione IV*, 1965
              E. *Actions for Six*, 1965

97. Raxach, Enrique
              A. *Estrofas*, 1963
              B. *Tientos*, 1967

98. Razzi, Fausto
              Improvvisazione III, 1968

99. Regamey, Constantin
              Autographe, 1967

100. Reynolds, Roger
              A. *Acquaintances*, 1963
              B. *Etudes, 4 flutes*, 1963
              C. *Mosaic*, 1963
              D. *The Emperor of Ice Cream*, 1963
              E. *Wedge*, 1963

101. Risatti, Howard
              A. *Sillabe #2*, 1972
              B. *Spectres*, 1972
              C. *Piccoli Pezzi*, 1971
              D. *Quartet #2*, 1971
              E. *Quartet #1*, 1971
              F. *Sillabe #1*, 1971
              G. *Symphony*, 1970
              H. *Etude*, 1972

102. Rochberg, George
              Blake Songs, 1963

103. Rosenbloom, D.
              And Come Up Dripping, 1969

104. Rudzinski, Zbigniew
              A. *Contra Fidem*, 1965
              B. *Trio Smyczkowe*, 1965

105. Schäffer, Boguslaw
              A. *Scultura*, 1967
              B. *Collage + Form*, 1965
              C. *Musica Ipsa*, 1965
              D. *Course "J"*, 1964
              E. *Topofonica*, 1962

106. Schiller, Henryk
              Inventions for Orchestra, 1963

107. Schoenberg, Arnold
    A. *De Profundis*, 1953
    B. *Pierrot Lunaire*, 1914

108. Schönbach, Dieter
    Lyrische Gesänge II, 1964

109. Schwantner, Joseph
    Chronicon, 1968

110. Sculthorpe, Peter
    Irkanda IV, 1967

111. Serocki, Kazimierz
    A. *Freski Symfoniczne*, 1966
    B. *Segmenti*, 1962
    C. *Epizody*, 1961
    D. *Musica Concertante*, 1960
    E. *Serce Nocy*, 1959

112. Shallenberg, Frank R.
    Lilacs, 1967

113. Shapey, Ralph
    A. *String Quartet #1*
    B. *String Quartet #5*
    C. *For Solo Trumpet*, 1967

114. Stevenson, Ronald
    Prelude, Fugue, and Fantasy on Busoni's Faust, 1967

115. Stiller, Andrew
    Electronic Construction

116. Stockhausen, Karlheinz
    A. *Klavierstücke X*, 1967
    B. *Kontakte Nr. 12*, 1966
    C. *Klavierstücke VIII*, 1965
    D. *Punkte (1952-62)*, 1963
    E. *Refrain*, 1961

117. Subotnick, Morton
    Serenade #3 for flute, 1965

118. Szabelski, Boleslaw
    A. *Koncert na flet i orkiestre*, 1968
    B. *Preludia*, 1964

119. Szalonek, Witold
    A. *Quattro Monologhi*, 1968
    B. *Les Sons*, 1967
    C. *Concertino*, 1965

120. Takahashi, Yuji
    Six Stoecheia, 1969

121. Valcárcel, Edgar
            Dicotomia III, 1968

122. Varèse, Edgar
            A. *Hyperprism* (1924), 1961
            B. *Ecuatorial* (1933-34), 1961
            C. *Déserts* (1951-54), 1959
            D. *Offrandes* (1921-22), 1929

123. Veretti, Antonio
            Priere Pour Demander Une Étoile, 1967

124. Vostřák, Zbyněk
            Pendel der Zeit, 1968

125. Webern, Anton
            Quintet for Piano and Strings, 1962

126. Wilkinson, Marc
            Voices from "Waiting for Godot," 1960

127. Wirtel, Thomas
            Music for Winds, Percussion, and Prepared Piano

128. Wolff, Christian
            A. *For 5 or 10 People*, 1963
            B. *Suite I*, 1963
            C. *Summer*, 1962

129. Wuorinen, Charles
            Flute Variations, 1967

130. Xenakis, Iannis
            A. *Syrmos*, 1968
            B. *Metastáseis*, 1967
            C. *Pithoprakta*, 1967
            D. *Morsima-Amorsima* (1956-62), 1967
            E. *Nomos*, 1967
            F. *ST/10-1,080262*, 1967

131. Zimmermann, Bernd-Alois
            Monologe (1960/4)

BIBLIOGRAPHY

Bartolozzi, Bruno. *New Sounds for Woodwind*. Trans. and ed. Reginald Smith Brindle. London: Oxford University Press, 1967.

Brown, E. "Notation und Ausführung Neuer Musik," *Darmstädter Beiträge zur Neuen Musik*, n9:64-86, 1965.

Cardew, C. "Notation—Interpretation, etc. (Experimental Music)" *Tempo*, n58: 21-33 (Summer), 1961.

Caskel, C. "Notationen für Schlagzeug," *Darmstädter Beiträge zur Neuen Musik*, n9:110-116, 1965.

Dahlhaus, C. "Notenschrift heute," *Darmstädter Beiträge zur Neuen Musik*, n9:9-34, 1965.

Fawcett, R. *Equiton*. Zurich: R. Fawcett, 1958.

Fuller, C. M. "A Music Notation Based on E and G," *Journal of Research in Music Education*, 14:193-96 (n3), 1966.

Hastings, M. D. "Will 'Klavarscribo' Work? New Notation discussed at I.S.M. Conference," *Musical Opinion*, 88:275 (February), 1965.

Haubenstock-Ramati, R. "Notation—Material and Form," *Darmstädter Beiträge zur Neuen Musik*, n9:51-54, 1965.

Kagel, M. "Komposition—Notation—Interpretation," *Darmstädter Beiträge zur Neuen Musik*, n9:55-63, 1965.

Karkoschka, E. "Ich habe mit Equiton komponiert," *Melos*, 29:232-39 (July-August), 1962.

_____. "Darmstadt hilft der Notation neuer Musik," *Melos*, 33:76-85 (March), 1966.

_____. *Das Schriftbild der Neuen Music*. Celle: Hermann Moeck, 1966.

Kontarsky, A. "Notationen für Klavier," *Darmstädter Beiträge zur Neuen Musik*, n9:92-109, 1965.

Ligeti, G. "Neue Notation—Kommunikationsmittel oder Selbstzweck?" *Darmstädter Beiträge zur Neuen Musik*, n9:35-50, 1965.

Lin, E. "The Notation for Continuous Gradual Change of Pitch," *Journal of International Folk Music Council*, 16:107-108, 1964.

Linger, B. L. "An Experimental Study of Durational Notation." *Dissertation Abstracts, Section A: The Humanities and Social Sciences*. Ann Arbor, Mich.: University Microfilms Inc., 1966.

Martino, D. "Notation in General—Articulation in Particular," *Perspectives of New Music*, 4:47-58 (n2), 1966.

Mathews, M. V., and L. Rosler. "Graphical Language for the Scores of Computer-generated Sounds," *Perspectives of New Music*, 6:92-118 (n2), 1968.

Mayer, H. "Musikale Grafica (Actiescrift)," *Mens En Mel*, 18:276-80 (September), 1964.

McElheran, B. "Preparing Stockhausen's 'Momente,'" *Perspectives of New Music*, 4:33-38 (n1), 1965.

O'Conner, G. A. "Prevailing Trends in Contemporary Percussion Notation," *Percussionist*, 3:61-74 (n4), 1966.

Otte, H. "Neue Notationen und ihre Folgen," *Melos*, 28:76-78 (March), 1961.

"Percussive Arts Society: Project on Terminology and Notation of Percussion Instruments," *Percussionist*, 3:47-53 (n2-3), 1966.

Poné, G. "Action-Reaction," *The Music Review*, 27:218-27 (n3), 1966.

Pooler, F., and Brent Pierce. *New Choral Notation*. New York: Walton Music Corp., 1971.

Read, G. *Music Notation: A Manual of Modern Practice*. Boston: Allyn & Bacon, 1964.

Roschitz, K. "Zur Notation neuen Musik-Anmerkungen über Grundsätze, Methoden, Zeichen," *Österreichische Musikzeitschrift*, 22:189-205 (April), 1967.

Stephan, R[udolf]. *Notationen im 20. Jahrhundert*. Sonderdruck aus: *Die Musik in Geschichte und Gegenwart* 9. Kassel, 1961.

Stockhausen, K. "Musik und Graphik," *Darmstädter Beiträge zur Neuen Musik*, n3:5-25, 1960.

Stone, K. "Problems and Methods of Notation," *Perspectives of New Music*, 1:9-31 (n2), 1963.

_____. Review of Karkoschka, *Das Schriftbild der Neuen Musik*, in *Perspectives of New Music*, 5:146-54 (n2), 1967.

Thomas, E. *Notation Neuer Musik*. Mainz: B. Schott, 1965. Reviewed in *Musica*, 20:197-78, 1966.

What is Klavarskribo? Slikkerveer, The Netherlands: The Klavarskribo Institute, 1947.

INDEX